CHATS ON COSTUME

CHATS ON COSTUME

GEORGE WOOLLISCROFT RHEAD

ISBN: 978-93-5420-848-5

Published: 1906

LECTOR HOUSE LLP

LECTOR HOUSE LLP
E-MAIL: lectorpublishing@gmail.com

PORTRAIT OF MISS ELLEN TERRY AS "LADY MACBETH,"
BY J. S. SARGENT, R.A.

(Reproduced by kind permission of the Artist.)

CHATS ON COSTUME

BY

G. WOOLLISCROFT RHEAD, R.E.

AUTHOR OF "THE TREATMENT OF DRAPERY IN ART," "THE PRINCIPLES
OF DESIGN," "A HANDBOOK OF ETCHING," "STUDIES IN
PLANT FORM," ETC., ETC.

WITH 117 ILLUSTRATIONS,
INCLUDING 35 LINE DRAWINGS BY THE AUTHOR

HORNED HEAD-DRESS: BEATRICE, COUNTESS OF ARUNDEL, 1439.

1906

PREFACE

Needless to say the present work is far from exhausting the subject of costume, which extends, indeed, over the whole field of history. For reasons of space, neither ecclesiastical nor military costume is touched upon. The book makes no pretensions to being anything more than what its title suggests—a series of chats upon a subject which fills a considerable place in the minds of, at any rate, the larger half of the community.

While many works germane to the subject of costume have, of necessity, been here largely drawn upon in the way of quotation, there will, at the same time, be found a certain proportion of what may be described as fresh material, the result of the author's acquaintance with the subject in his individual practice as an artist. Indeed, the subject of dress is, or should be, an artistic matter; it was so in the past, and it will again, in the very near future, come to be recognised as one of the Decorative Arts, requiring artistic knowledge, and some perception of the fundamental laws of Design.

The author's thanks are particularly due to Mr. J. S. Sargent, R.A., for his kind permission to reproduce his portrait of Miss Ellen Terry.

WILLIAM, DUKE OF JULIERS AND CLEVES (ALDEGREVER).

By Aldegrever.

BIBLIOGRAPHY

Anglo-Saxon Chronicle.

Barclay: Ship of Fools of the World, 1508.

Bell's Fashionable Magazine, 1812.

Bulwer: Pedigree of the English Gallant.

Carlyle, T.: Sartor Resartus; French Revolution.

Caxton: The Four Sons of Aymon.

Chaucer.

English Costume from Pocket-books, 1799.

Eginhart: Life of Charlemagne, 1619.

Fairholt: Costume in England, 1896.

Froissart's Chronicles, H. N. Humphreys, 1855.

Gregory of Tours: History of the Franks.

Gosson, Stephen: Schoole of Abuse, 1579.

Harding's Chronicle, 1543.

Holme, Randal: Notes on Dress, *c.* 1660.

Hope, T.: Costume of the Ancients.

Jonson, Ben: Plays.

John de Meun
William de Lorris] Romance of the Rose.

Knight of La Tour Landry, 1371, Caxton.

Lydgate, Monk of Bury: Poems.

Le Blanc, H., Esq.: The Art of Tying the Cravat, 1828.

Paris, Matthew.

Piers Plowman: Pierce Ploughman's Vision.

Planché: British Costume, 1874; Cyclopædia of Costume, 1877.

Racinet: Costume.

Roxburghe Ballads, *c.* 1686.

Statutes: Henry III., Henry VIII.

Stothard, C.: Monumental Effigies, 1877.

Strutt: Dress and Habits of the English People, 1842.

Stubbes: Anatomy of Abuses.

Stow, John: Chronicle, 1615.

Stewart, J.: Plocacosmos, or the Whole Art of Hairdressing, 1782.

Viollet le Duc: Dictionnaire raisonné du mobilier Français, 1858-75.

Wright, T.: Caricature and History of the Georges, 1868.

William of Malmesbury.

CONTENTS

LIST OF ILLUSTRATIONS

I
A GENERAL SURVEY

"You see two individuals, one dressed in fine Red, the other in coarse threadbare Blue: Red says to Blue: 'Be hanged and anatomised;' Blue hears with a shudder, and (O wonder of wonders!) marches sorrowfully to the gallows; is there noosed-up, vibrates his hour, and the surgeons dissect him, and fit his bones into a skeleton for medical purposes. How is this; or what make ye of your Nothing can act but where it is? Red has no physical hold of Blue, no clutch of him, is nowise in contact with him: neither are those ministering Sheriffs and Lord-Lieutenants and Hangmen and Tipstaves so related to commanding Red, that he can tug them hither and thither; but each stands distinct within his own skin. Nevertheless as it is spoken so it is done; the articulated Word sets all hands in action; and Rope and Improved-drop perform their work.

"Thinking reader, the reason seems to me twofold: First, that man is a Spirit, and bound by invisible bonds to All Men; secondly, that he wears Clothes, which are the visible emblems of that fact. Has not your Red hanging-individual a horsehair wig, squirrel-skins and a plush-gown; whereby all mortals know that he is a Judge?—Society, which the more I think of it astonishes me the more, is founded upon Cloth."

Carlyle, Sartor Resartus.

CHATS ON COSTUME

I

A GENERAL SURVEY

That singular clothes-philosopher, Diogenes Teufelsdröckh, whose revolutionary theories upon the subject of the "vestural tissue" first burst upon an astonished world some seventy odd years ago, has, with characteristic emphasis, drawn attention, amongst other things, to the fact that man is the only animal who is not provided with some Nature-made protection against the elements—a protection either of fur, feather, hide, or what not. Bounteous Nature, however, always kind, who never withholds a good without affording ample compensation, has endowed man with that fertile brain and cunning hand whereby he may convert hide into leather, wool of sheep into cloth, web of worm into silk, flax and cotton into linen of various kinds, and so restore that balance of endowment without which man would be at the mercy of every wind that blew.

The uses of clothes, or costume—the words may be here taken as synonymous—may be said to be threefold: first, for decency, which was their first and apparently only use, as we may assume that in Eden the sun always shone; secondly, for comfort and protection; thirdly, for beauty and adornment.

First, then, for decency. That is sufficiently clearly established if we may accept the Mosaic account of the world's juvenescence: "And the eyes of both of them were opened, and they knew that they were naked; and they sewed fig leaves together, and made themselves aprons"; "Unto Adam also and to his wife did the Lord God make coats of skins and clothed them."[1] This habit of observance of the

---

[1] Gen. iii. 7, 21.

decencies of life appears to be common to all nations. No people or tribe, however primitive the civilisation, but makes some sort of provision in this respect. The Veddas of Ceylon make girdles of leaves, which gives them a strangely fantastic appearance. We learn from the accounts of travellers in Central Africa that "clothing, though extremely simple, consisting of a little grass-cloth, ornaments of feathers, fur, shells, glass and metal beads, are worn, and the skin is decorated by stripes of paint or an extensive series of cicatrices." Among the aborigines of the Malay Peninsula (Sakais) "the men wear a strip of bark-cloth twisted round the waist and drawn between the legs. The women sometimes wear small cotton-cloth petticoats (sarongs) purchased from the Malays, and the men occasionally adopt Chinese trousers; but in their native forests, however, none of these luxuries are indulged in."

THE COMTE D'ARTOIS AND MADEMOISELLE CLOTHILDE.

Secondly, for comfort and protection. The climatic influence on dress is, and must necessarily be, considerable. This is well illustrated by the well-known fable of "The Wind and the Sun." The more boisterously the wind blows, the more closely the man enwraps himself with his cloak; the more fiercely the sun shines, the more the man divests himself of raiment;[2] but between the skins of the Lap-lander, fashioned by the help of a thorn or a fishbone for a needle, and the sinews of the animal for thread, and the light gossamer clothing of the countries of the East there is a vast range, the extent of which, indeed, is almost boundless. Climate not only determines the amount or degree of warmth or otherwise, but also, as in architecture, influences its character both as to form and colour. Moreover, clothes are an index to the character or temper of an individual or nation. "What meaning lies in Colour! If the Cut betoken intellect and talent, so does the Colour betoken temper and heart."[3]

CHARLES HOWARD, EARL OF NOTTINGHAM.

Engraved by Thomas Cockson.

[2] This fable is so quaintly told in Lyly's "Euphues" (1580), that it may be worth while to repeat it. "A gentleman walking abroad, the Winde thought to blowe of(f) his cloake, which with great blastes and blustering striving to vnloose it, made it to stick faster to his backe, for the more the winde encreased the closer his cloake clapt to his body, then the Sunne, shining with his hoat beames began to warme this gentleman, who waxing som(e) what faint in this faire weather, did not on(e)ly put of(f) his cloake but his coate, which the Wynde perceiuing, yeelded the conquest to the Sunne."

[3] Carlyle, "Sartor Resartus."

Thirdly, for beauty and adornment—and it is with this latter aspect that this work is mainly concerned. That clothes *should* be beautiful is an axiom which, one would think, might readily be accepted; that clothes *have been* beautiful is a fact which cannot be denied. (It is only during the present utilitarian age that the æsthetic principle has been lost sight of.) That clothes *might again* be beautiful, without suffering any loss on the score of utility, is also unquestionable. To attempt to follow the whims and vagaries of that jade, Fashion, through all her endless diversities and constant changes, would indeed be a Herculean task, and might well appal the boldest he (or she, for that matter) who would wield pen or pencil.

The will-o'-the-wisp of Fashion is, however, a less capricious person than would appear at first sight. There is some method in her madness. Similar types, similar decorative *motifs*, appear and reappear through the centuries with the regularity of the changing seasons. The veracious chronicler may therefore take some comfort from this fact; it lightens his burden, and makes his task less difficult than it would otherwise be. Moreover, dress, as in architectural form, to the careful student of decorative development, presents really less inherent variety than one would suppose; historical accuracy is the favourite bugbear of pedants, and, while appreciating to the full the great distinctiveness of such periods as the Elizabethan, the Stuart, and the Georgian, there are certain primitive forms, certain leading characteristics, which are common to most periods, and which, like the poor, are always with us. One might hazard the contention that a painter would be perfectly safe in introducing a pot-hat and a pair of trousers at practically any period of the world's history—*not in conjunction, mind*; no, that glorious consummation was reserved for this happy age of ours. The Greeks, however, as is well known, wore trousers. Some form of the trouser was worn by the lower classes at most periods of English history. Ben Jonson makes Peniboy junior walk in his "gowne, waistcoate, and *trouses*," expecting his tailor. Nay, do we not read in the Old Testament—in *some* Old Testaments, at any rate—that even Adam and Eve made themselves—ahem!—breeches? As for the pot-hat, its origin is lost in the maze of antiquity. It crops up in its various developments at all sorts of odd times and periods. A fearsome variety of it is to be seen upon the head of Jan Arnolfini in Van Eyck's picture in the National Gallery. It appears in Durer's engravings and woodcuts, woolly, hairy structures, occasionally of abnormal height. It is perhaps not generally known that it occurs in the Raphael cartoons ("Paul preaching at Athens"). One would have imagined such a singular appearance as a pot-hat, in such surroundings, to have been evident at first sight. The reason it was not so was on account of its colour (vermilion). Had it been black, one would have spotted it at once; and this fact, when one comes to consider it, is a little singular, since, if one were to march down Piccadilly some fine afternoon crowned in a vermilion pot-hat, methinks one would not *altogether* escape notice.

There is, however, still another aspect of clothes which remains to be considered, *i.e.*, their symbolism. It has been written, "Manners maketh man." It might also be written with even a still greater degree of truth, "*Clothes* maketh man," since clothes contribute so much to man's dignity. Carlyle finds it difficult to imagine a naked Duke of Windlestraw addressing a naked House of Lords, and asks, very pertinently, "Who ever saw any Lord my-lorded in tattered blanket fastened with a wooden skewer?" His King Toom-tabard (empty gown) reigning over Scotland long after the man John Baliol had gone! His quaint conceit of a suit of cast clothes, meekly bearing its honours, without haughty looks or scornful gesture, has been imitated by Thackeray in his amusing illustration of "Ludovicus Rex" — the "silent dignity" of "Rex" as represented by the suit of clothes, the forlorn appearance of Ludovicus, the magnificence of "Ludovicus Rex," all testify to the great importance and value of costume, as contrasted with the relatively trivial character of the wearer.

"LUDOVICUS REX , BY THACKERAY."

From "Paris Sketches."

Who, then, shall dare to belittle the importance of costume? or to affirm that character can rise superior to its environment? Our subject is one of the most significant which can be presented to the reader's consideration. It provides one of the most curious and fascinating studies in the world.

The materials upon which we base our knowledge of the dress of the earlier periods of the world's history are necessarily scanty. For the Egyptian and Assyrian period we are dependent upon monumental inscriptions and carving, and the few papyri which have survived the ravages of time. For the Greek and Roman period, upon sculpture, pottery, and the written description of the more considerable authors. For the Byzantine, Frankish, and Gothic periods, upon mosaic, monumental effigies, and illuminated MSS. It is not until what may be called the age of the *painter* that we may be said to emerge into the broad light of day, and the pencils of Holbein, Rubens, and Vandyke make things clearer for us. The sumptuary laws, however, enacted at various periods, against excess in apparel and extravagance in dress, let in a flood of light on the manners and customs of the times, and in them will be found many curious and interesting details. The principal Acts are the following: 2 Edw. II. c. 4; 37 Edw. III. cc. 8, 14; 3 Edw. IV. c. 1; 22 Edw. IV. c. 1; 1 Hen. VIII. c. 14; 6 Hen. VIII. c. 1; 7 Hen. VIII. c. 6; 24 Hen. VIII. c. 13; 1 and 2 Phil. and Mary, c. 2; 8 Eliz. c. 11. All these laws were repealed by an Act of 1 Jac. I.

This grandmotherly legislation, which was never effective, always evaded and even defied, had a double object in view, first to induce habits of thrift amongst all classes of the people, and secondly on æsthetic grounds.

In the thirty-seventh year of the reign of Edward III. (A.D. 1363), the Commons exhibited a complaint in Parliament against the general usage of expensive apparel not suited either to the degree or income of the people; and an Act was passed by which the following regulations were insisted upon: Furs of ermine and lettice, and embellishments of pearls, excepting for a head-dress, were strictly forbidden to any but the Royal Family, and nobles possessing upwards of £1,000 per annum.

Cloths of gold and silver, and habits embroidered with jewellery, lined with pure miniver, and other expensive furs, were permitted only to knights and ladies, whose incomes exceeded 400 marks yearly.

Knights whose income exceeded 200 marks, or squires possessing £200 in lands or tenements, were permitted to wear cloth of silver with ribands, girdles, &c., reasonably embellished with silver, and woollen cloth, of the value of six marks the whole piece; but all persons under the rank of knighthood, or of less property than the last mentioned, were confined to the use of cloth not exceeding four marks the piece, and were prohibited wearing silks and embroidered garments of any sort, or embellishing their apparel with any ornaments of gold, silver, or jewellery. Rings, buckles, ouches, girdles, and ribands were forbidden them, and the penalty annexed to the infringement of this statute was the forfeiture of the dress or ornament so made or worn.

In the reign of Henry IV. these laws were so little regarded that it was found necessary to revive them with considerable additions. It was enacted that—"No man not being a banneret, or person of high estate," was permitted to wear cloth of gold, of crimson, or cloth of velvet, or motley velvet, or large hanging sleeves open or closed, or gowns so long as to touch the ground, or to use the furs of ermine, lettice, or marten, excepting only "gens d'armes quant ils sont armez." Decorations of gold and silver were forbidden to all who possessed less than £200 in goods and chattels, or £20 per annum, unless they were heirs to estates of 50 marks per annum, or to £500 worth of goods and chattels.

Four years afterwards it was ordained that no man, let his condition be what it might, should be permitted to wear a gown or garment cut or slashed into pieces in the form of letters, rose leaves, and posies of various kinds, or any such-like devices, under the penalty of forfeiting the same, and the offending tailor was to be imprisoned during the King's pleasure.

In the third year of the reign of Edward IV. an Act was promulgated by which cloth of gold, cloth of silk of a purple colour, and fur of sables were prohibited to all knights under the estate of lords. Bachelor knights were forbidden to wear cloth of velvet upon velvet, unless they were Knights of the Garter; and simple esquires, or gentlemen, were restricted from the use of velvet, damask, or figured satin, or any counterfeit resembling such stuffs, except they possessed a yearly income to the value of £100, or were attached to the King's Court or household.

It was also forbidden to any persons who were not in the enjoyment of £40 yearly income to wear any of the richer furs; also girdles of gold, silver, or silver-gilt were forbidden.

No one under the estate of a lord was permitted to wear indecently short jackets, gowns, &c., mentioned by Monstrelet, or pikes or poleines to his shoes and boots exceeding two inches in length. No yeoman, or person under the degree of a yeoman, was allowed bolsters or stuffing of wool, cotton, or cadis in his purpoint or doublet under a penalty of six shillings and eightpence fine, and forfeiture awarded; the unfortunate tailor making such short or stuffed dresses, or shoemaker manufacturing such long-toed shoes for unprivileged persons, being under the pain of cursing by the clergy for the latter offence, as well as the forfeit of twenty shillings—one noble to the King, another to the cordwainers of London, and the third to the Chamber of London.

It will readily be seen that these laws were necessarily the cause of great hindrance to trade, which was, indeed, not the least of the evils occasioned by these absurd laws. Richard Onslow, Recorder of London, 1565 (given in Ellis's "Original Letters," vol. ii.), describes an interview which he had with the civic tailors, who were puzzled to know whether they might "line a slop-hose not cut in panes, with a lining of cotton stitched to the slop, over and besydes the linen lining straight to the leg."

The statutory laws, however, were not the *only* hindrance to trade, since it would appear that during the Plantagenet period *dishonesty* in trade was as rife as it is at the present time, and foreign competition as keen; the conditions, however, were slightly different, the foreign merchants obtaining high prices for their goods, instead of dumping cheap goods into the country at low prices. The remedy was directed to the enforcement of greater honesty in trade dealings, rather than to fortify themselves behind tariff walls.

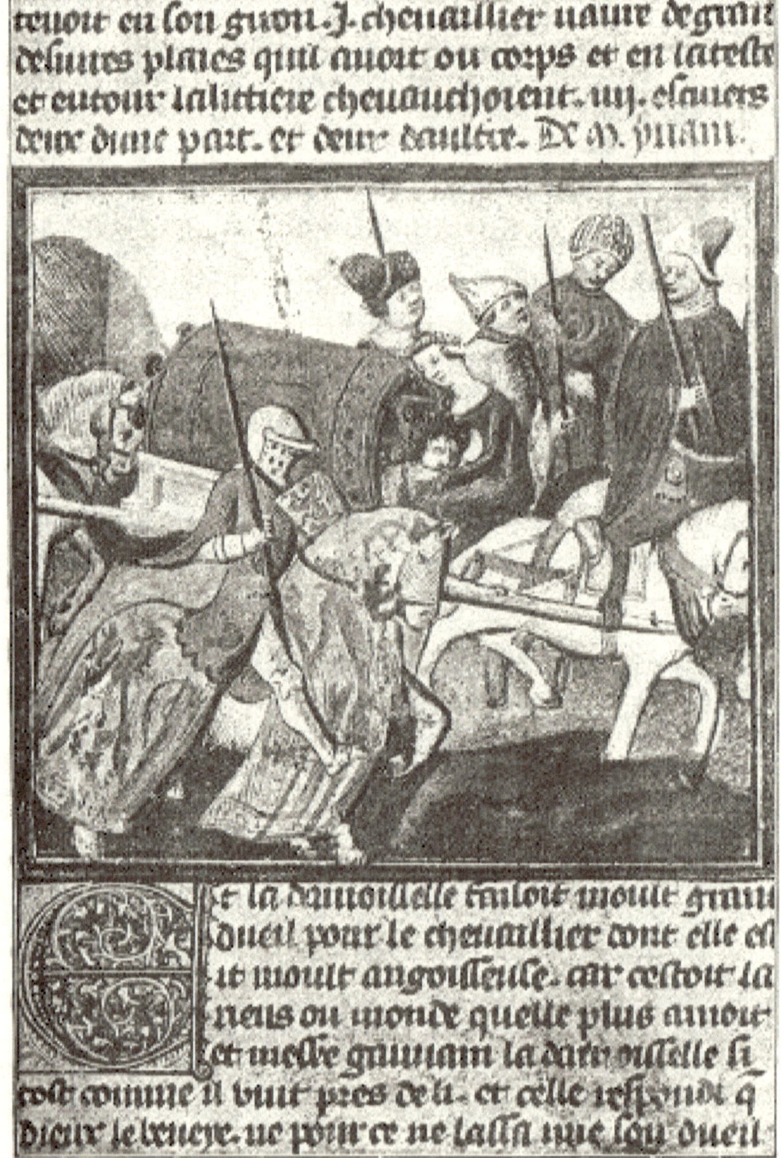

**TRAVELLING IN A HORSE LITTER
(FROM A FOURTEENTH CENTURY MS.).**

*From the MS. 118 Français in the Bibliothèque Nationale
(late Fourteenth Century).*

It was enacted in the third year of the reign of Edward IV. c. 1:—"Firste,
whereas many yeres paste & nowe at this daye, the workemanshyp of clothes &

things requisite to the same, is & hath bene of such fraude disceite & falsite, that the sayde clothes in other landes & countreis, is had in small reputacyon, to the greate shame of this lande. And by reason thereof a great quantite of clothes of other strange landes be brought into this realme, & here solde at an highe & excessyve pryce, evydently shewynge thossens defaulte & falsyte of the maykynge of wollen clothes of this lande. Our soveraigne lorde the Kynge, for the remedy of the premisses, & to the preferment of such labours & occupacions, which hath been used by the makynge of the sayde clothes, by thaduyse assent & request & auctoritie aforsayd, hath ordeyned & establysshed, that every hole wollen clothe called brodclothe, which shal be made & set to sale after the feaste of Saynt Peter called ad vincula, which shal be in the yere of our Lorde M.CCCC.LXV. after the ful waterynge & rackyng straynyng or tenturyng of the same redy to sale, shall holde & conteyne in length xxiiii yardes, & to every yarde an ynche, conteynynge the bredthe of a mannes ynche, to be measured by the creste of the same clothe. And i brede ii yardes, or vii quarters at the leaste wythyn the lystes. & if the clothe be longer in measure than xxiiii yardes & the ynches than the byer therof shall paye to the seller for for as moche as doth excede such measure of xxiiii yardes, after the rate of the measure above ordeyned. Also it is ordeined & establisshed by auctoritie of the sayd lordes, that all maner clothes called streytes, to be made & put to sale after the same feaste, after the full watering & rackyng, streynynge or tenturynge therof redye to sale, shall holde & conteyne in lengthe xii yardes & the ynches, after the measure aforsaid, & in brede one yarde within the lystes. Also it is ordeyned & establysshed by thauctoritie aforsaid, that every clothe called kersey, to be made & put to sale after the sayde feaste, after the full waterynge & rackynge straynynge or tenturynge of the same redy to sale, shall holde & conteyne in lengthe xviii yardes & the ynches, as is aforsayd, & in brede one yarde & a nayle, or at the leaste one yarde within the lystes. & also it is ordeyned & establysshed, that every halfe clothe of every of the sayde hole clothes, streytes, & kerseys, shall kepe his measure in length & brede after the rate fourme & nature of his hole clothe aforsayde. & that no persone, whiche shall make or cause to be made any maner wollen clothe to sel after the said feaste shall medle or put in or upon the same cloth, nor the wolle, whereof the sayd clothe shall be made, any lambes wolle, flockes or corke in any maner, upon payne to forfayt xxs. for every clothe or halfe clothe, wherein & wherupon any such lambes wolle, flockes or corke shall be put or medled. The one halfe thereof to be to the Kyng, & the other halfe to hym that shall leyse the same clothe, & duely prove the same to be made contrarie to this ordinance, excepte that he shall chose to make of lambes wolle by itselfe without mynglyng with any other wolle. Excepte also that corke may be used in dyenge upon woded wolle, & also in dyenge of all suche clothe, that is onely made of woded wolle, so that the same wolle & clothe be perfytly boyled & madered, except also that corke may be put upon clothe, whiche is perfectly boyled & madered"—but enough of this. The sumptuary laws continued to be enacted against this, that, or the other abuse, or fancied abuse. If a new fashion sprung up, a brand new law would be immediately fashioned for the purpose of keeping it within bounds. It was to no purpose, however; the sumptuary laws continued to be disregarded as heretofore. "How often hath her majestie with the grave advice

of her honorable Councell, sette downe the limits of apparell to every degree, &
how soon again hath the pride of our harts overflowen the chanell!"[4]

GUILJELMUS III.
D. G. ANGLIÆ, SCOTIÆ, FRANCIÆ et HIBERNIÆ REX.

WILLIAM III.

It was the same with the satirists, whether of horned head-dresses or other
extravagances; Monk Lydgate might rave, might shout himself hoarse, but the
women would have their horns.

It was indeed inevitable that the vagaries of fashion and the love of fine feathers should become the favourite butt of the satirists, purists, and other persons
who assumed the character of mentor. Among the most insistent of these were the
priesthood. St. Bernard thus admonishes his sister, perhaps with greater candour

[4] Stephen Gosson, "The School of Abuse."

than politeness, on her visiting him, "well arraied with riche clothing, with perles and precious stones":—

"Suster, yet ye love youre bodi, by reson ye shuld beter love youre soule: wene ye not that ye displese God and his aungels to see in you suche pompe and pride to adorn suche a carion as is youre body.... Whi thenke ye not that the pore peple that deyen for hungir and colde, that for the sixte part of youre gay arraye xl per- sones might be clothed, refresshed, and kepte from the colde?... And thanne the ladi wepte, and solde awey her clothes, and levid after an holy lyff, and had love of God, aungeles, and holy seintes, the whiche is beter thanne of the worldely pepille" ("Knight of La Tour Landry," 1371).

The sister of St. Bernard, however, evidently lacked the power of repartee of St. Edith, daughter of King Edgar, who, though brought up in a convent at Wilton, and destined to the life of the cloister, nevertheless had a weakness for clothes which seemed too fine and gay for a nun. St. Ethelwold, who, it is clear, must have shared the opinions of St. Bernard upon the subject of finery, and ventured to up- braid her, received this crushing reply: "God's doom, that may not fail, is pleased only with conscience. Therefore I trow that as clean a soul may be under those clothes that are arrayed with gold as under thy slight fur-skins." He was reminded also that St. Augustine had said that pride could lurk even in rags. This latter sally calls to mind the story of Diogenes spitting upon the floor of Plato's house and ex- claiming, "Thus I trample on the pride of Plato." "With *greater* pride, O Diogenes," was the quiet rejoinder.

Dowglas, the monk of Glastonbury, writing against the extravagances which were rife during the latter half of the reign of Edward III., says: "The English haunted so much unto the foly of strangers, that every year they changed them in diverse shapes and disguisings of clothing, now long, now large, now wide, now strait, and every day clothingges, new and destitute, and devest from all honesty of old arraye or good usage; and another time in short clothes, and so strait waist- ed, with full sleeves and tapetes of surcoats and hodes, over long and large, all so ragged and knib on every side, and all so shattered, and also buttoned, that I with truth shall say, they seem more like to tormentors or devils in their clothing, and also in their shoying and other arraye than they seemed to be like men."

The authors of the "Roman de la Rose," William de Lorris, who died in 1260, and John de Meun, who continued and finished the poem about 1304, are amongst the most severe of these satirists. In alluding to the unnecessary length of their trains, the author advises the ladies, if their legs be not handsome, nor their feet small and delicate, to wear long robes trailing on the pavement to hide them; those having pretty feet are counselled to elevate their robes, as if for air and conve- nience, that all who are passing may see and admire. This has been imitated by Ben Jonson, who in his "Silent Woman" makes Truewit say:—

"I love a good dressing before any beauty o' the world. Oh, a woman is then like a delicate garden; nor is there one kind of it; she may vary every hour; take often counsel of her glass, and choose the best. If she have good ears, show them; good hair, lay it out; good legs, wear short clothes; a good hand, discover it often;

practise any art to mend breath, cleanse teeth, repair eyebrows, paint, and profess it."

Maria

D. G. Angliæ, Scotiæ, Franciæ et Hiberniæ Regina.

QUEEN MARY.

The author of the "Roxburghe Ballads" ("A Woman's Birth and Education") informs us that when Cupid first beheld a woman—

"He prankt it up in Fardingals and Muffs,
In Masks, Rebatos, Shapperowns, and Wyers,
In Paintings, Powd'rings, Perriwigs, and Cuffes,
In Dutch, Italian, Spanish, French attires;
Thus was it born, brought forth, and made Love's baby,
And this is that which now we call a Lady."

Nor was it the fair sex only who were thus lampooned. The men also came in for their share, and were as much the objects of the satirist's wrath as were the women: —

> "Your ruffs and your bands,
> And your cuffs at your hands,
> Your pipes and your smokes,
> And your short curtall clokes,
> Scarfes, feathers and swerdes,
> And their bodkin beards;
> Your wastes a span long,
> Your knees with points hung
> Like morrice-dance bels
> And many toyes els."

SKELTON, Elinor Rummin, 1625.

The Knight of La Tour Landry, writing towards the close of the fourteenth century, in order to deter his daughters from extravagance and superfluity of dress, recounts a story of a knight who, having lost his wife, applied to "an heremyte hys uncle" to know whether she was saved or not and how it "stode with her." The hermit, after many prayers, dreamed that he saw "Seint Michelle & the develle that had her in a balaunce, & alle her good dedes in the same balaunce, & a develle & alle her evelle dedes in that other balaunce. & the most that grevid her was her good & gay clothing, & furres of gray menivere & letuse; & the develle cried & sayde, Seint Michel, this woman had tenne diverse gownes & as mani cotes; & thou wost welle lesse myghte have suffised her after the lawe of God; ... & he toke all her juellys and rynges, ... & also the false langage that she had saide ... & caste hem in the balaunce with her evelle dedes." The "evelle dedes passed the good, & weyed downe & overcame her good dedes. & there the develle toke her, & bare her away, & putte her clothes & aray brennyng in the flawme on her with the fire of helle, & kist her doune into the pitte of helle; ... & the pore soul cried, & made moche sorughe & pite ... but it boted not."

Lydgate, the famous monk of Bury, and one of the foremost poets of his time, was unwearying in his condemnation of the extravagances of dress, his pet aversion being the horned head-dresses which obtained during the York and Lancastrian period. In a "Ditty of Women's Horns," he unbosoms himself as follows: —

> "Clerkys recorde, by gret auctoryté,
> Hornes wer yove to bestys for dyffence;
> A thing contrarye to femynté,
> To be maad sturdy of resystence.
> But arche wives, egre in ther vyolence,
> Fers as tygres for to make affray
> They have despit, and ageyn concyence
> Lyst nat of pryde, then hornes cast away."

But the most insistent of all the satirists was Philip Stubbes, who wrote his "Anatomy of Abuses" in the reign of Elizabeth. In lampooning the feminine habit of aping masculine dress, he says: "The women have doublets and jerkins as the men have, buttoned up to the breast, and made with wings, welts, and pinions on the shoulder-points, as man's apparel in all respects; and although this be a kind of attire proper only to a man, yet they blush not to wear it."

Artists also, as well as writers, joined in the general chorus of condemnation of the extravagances of fashion. Strutt gives a cut from the MS. copy of Froissart in the Harleian Library, of a pig walking upon stilts playing the harp, and crowned with the high steeple head-dress which prevailed during the reign of Edward IV.

In the Cotton MS. (Nero, C4) there is an illustration of a winged devil arrayed in a costume with elongated sleeves tied in knots, the prevailing fashion of the period.

It must be confessed that the satirists were occasionally a little too severe in their strictures, for while doubtless extravagance prevailed at most periods—indeed, must always prevail—the dress of such a period as that of the Plantagenets, as well as that of Elizabeth, was sumptuous to a degree. In fact, it is difficult for us moderns, so surrounded as we are by commonness, cheapness, and vulgarity, to realise the extreme splendour of the Middle Ages, either as regards their dress or their surroundings. Plenty of extravagance there is at the present time, but no real magnificence, either as to invention or material.

CARICATURE: PIG WALKING UPON STILTS (HARLEIAN MS.) **CARICATURE: WINGED DEVIL (COTTON MS.)**

With respect to material, by far the most sumptuous fabric employed for purposes of adornment in past times is undoubtedly cloth of gold. This truly regal fabric has been in use from the earliest periods. "And they shall make the ephod of *gold*, of blue, and of purple, of scarlet, and fine twined linen, with cunning work. And the curious girdle of the ephod, which is upon it, shall be of the same, according to the work thereof; even of gold, of blue, and purple, and scarlet, and fine twined linen."[5]

It is recorded of the wife of the Emperor Honorius, who died about the year

[5] Exodus xxviii. 6-8.

400, upon the re-opening of her grave in 1544, the golden tissues which formed the shroud were melted, and amounted in weight to 36 lbs.

About the body of the Frankish King Childeric, when his grave was discovered in 1653, were found numerous strips of pure gold, pointing to the fact that the body must have been wrapped in a mantle of golden stuff for burial.

The sumptuary laws which were enacted at various periods of English history, regulating and restricting the wearing of this precious fabric to persons of estate, have already been referred to, and serve to show in what high estimation this fabric was held.

It will readily be imagined that cloth of gold was necessarily costly. The Princess Mary (afterwards Queen), thirteen years before she came to the throne, "Payed to Peycocke, of London, for xix yerds iii qrt of clothe of golde at xxxviijs. the yerde. xxxvij*li.* x*s.* vj*d.*" and for "a yerde & dr qrt of clothe of silver xls." In later times the use of the pure gold thread was discontinued except for very costly garments, and tissues were made of silver-gilt or copper-gilt thread. The thin paper which we now know by the name of tissue paper was originally made for the purpose of being placed between the pieces of stuff to prevent tarnishing when laid by.

Silk, like the sun, and so many other good things comes to us from the "sacred East." The earliest mention of it is in Aristotle, who refers to the importation into the Western world of raw silk. Silken garments were brought to Rome from a very early period, but on account of their costliness were worn only by a very few. Heliogabalus was the first Emperor who wore silk for clothing. By the revised code of laws issued for the Roman Empire in 533 A.D., a monopoly of silk weaving was given to the Court, looms being set up in the imperial palace and worked by women. The raw material, however, had still to be brought from abroad. The story of the introduction of the silkworm into Constantinople will serve to show how jealously the secret of the rearing of the worm was kept by the peoples of the East. The eggs of the silkworm were brought, hidden in their walking staves, by two Greek monks, who had lived many years amongst the Chinese and learnt the process of rearing the worm, and who carried them to Constantinople and presented them to the Emperor. Very soon afterwards the Western world reared its own silk.

Silk was known under different names at various periods, according to its colour, texture, or design. Samite, Samit, Examitum, is a six-threaded tissue, and consequently costly. The hand which grasped the sword Excalibur when it was thrown into the lake was clothed in white samite—

> "Launcelot and the Queen were cledde
> In robes of a rich wede,
> Of samyte white, with silver shredde."

Ciclatoun was a substance of light texture, and was used both for ecclesiastical purposes and for the more stately dresses of a secular character. Chaucer, in his "Rime of Sire Thopas," says:—

> "Of Brugges were his hosen broun
> His robe was of ciclatoun."

Cendal was a less costly fabric, and was also used largely in ecclesiastical vestments.

Taffeta was a thin transparent textile, and was used, as well as cendal, during the Middle Ages for linings.

Sarcenet also is a light webbed silk, and by degrees supplanted cendal.

Satin was also used in the Middle Ages, and is mentioned by Chaucer in his "Man of Lawe's Tale," but was not brought into general use until later. The beauties of the Court of Charles II., as pictured by Sir Peter Lely, are usually clad in satin.

Velvet, that most sumptuous material, has always been held in high estimation on account of the richness of its texture and fold. It has always been used, since its introduction into the West, for robes of state and for the more sumptuous kind of dress. The place of its origin is not known, but it probably comes from China.

DUCHESS OF ANCASTER (AFTER HUDSON).

In a letter preserved in the Record Office (*circa* 1505) to Edmund de la Pole, Earl of Suffolk, from his steward Killingworth (De la Pole had been indicted of homicide and murder, "for slaying of a mean person in his rage and fury," and had fled to Flanders), conveying excuses from some person un-named, mentioned only as "your friend," for not having communicated with De la Pole earlier, as he had hoped, to send him news from England, the writer continues:—

"For your gown he axked me howe many elles velvet wold serve you. I told hym xiiij Englishe yerdis, and then he saied, 'What lynyng thereunto?' I answerde 'Sarcenet' by cause of the lest coste to helpe it forward. And he saide to me, 'Wel, I shal see what I can doo therin.' Soo, sir, if it please you to write to him in Duche, and thank him, and geve but oon worde therin towching your gown, I doubte not ye shal have hyt."

The patternings of woven brocades, damasks and other textiles afford an interest quite apart from mere utility, or the purpose for which they were intended to serve as an ornamental adjunct to dress, since by their means we are able to trace the great ornamental traditions to their original source in the East.

The history of the art of weaving in China is lost in obscurity, but we may reasonably infer from our knowledge of the character of its people that neither their methods nor the character of the ornamentation have materially changed during a period of as much as two thousand years. Dionysius Periegetes informs us that the Seres "make precious figured garments resembling in colour the flowers of the field, and rivalling in fineness the work of spiders."

It is certain that the Egyptians practised the art of weaving from very early times, although the earliest ornamental fabrics found in Egypt are of the sixth century A.D. In later times, however, their woven fabrics were exceedingly sumptuous. Shakespeare's description of the barge of Cleopatra will be familiar to all—

> "The barge she sat in, like a burnished throne
> Burned on the water:
> Purple the sails, and so perfumed that
> The winds were love-sick with them; she did lie
> In her pavilion—cloth of gold, of tissue," &c.

The Sicilian brocades of the twelfth and thirteenth centuries were the finest in the world. The character of their ornamentation betrays their Eastern origin, and we may trace in them the various influences which were brought to bear upon them by their successive conquerors, and which left a lasting mark upon their art. The earliest ornamental influence was that of Byzantium, which followed upon the conquest of the island by Belisarius in 535. The patternings are made up of grotesque animals, birds, griffins, chimeras, &c., intertwined with conventional foliage or ornament of a purely abstract character. After the Saracen conquest, resultant upon the preaching of Muhammad, we find Arabic inscriptions freely introduced as part of the general decorative motive. Gold thread is lavishly used, and, together with an admixture of colour, usually forms the pattern, upon a coloured ground, dark or light, as the case may be.

**DAMASK IN SILK AND GOLD
(SARACENIC, ELEVENTH TO THIRTEENTH CENTURY).**

The tradition spread to the mainland of Italy, and looms were set up in Lucca, Florence, Venice, Genoa, and elsewhere; the character of the ornamentation gradually changing, however, as the Renascence influence began to make itself felt. Even the most cursory study of Italian painting will serve to give an idea of the splendour of the dresses of the Italian Gothic and Renascence periods.

VENETIAN FABRIC IN SILK AND GOLD (THIRTEENTH CENTURY).

It was Louis XI. who introduced the art of silk weaving into France, and looms were established at Tours in 1480. In 1520 looms were set up in Lyons by Francis I.

In England also the art of weaving flourished, and was employed for ecclesiastical vestments, hangings, furniture, and other purposes, as well as for civil dress. In the wardrobe accounts of Edward II. occurs the item: "To a mercer in London for a green hanging of wool with figures of Kings and Earls upon it, for the King's service in this hall on solemn feasts at London," &c.

For the "mantell of the Garter" of Henry VII. "a pound and a half of gold of Venys" was employed "aboute the making of a lace and boton."

Instances of the splendour of the costume at the different periods of the past might be multiplied indefinitely.

The monk of Malmesbury describes the banner under which Harold fought at Hastings as having been "embroidered in gold with the figure of a man in the act of fighting, studded with precious stones, woven sumptuously."

Chaucer describes the King's daughter in the "Squire of Low Degree" as having—

> "Mantell of ryche degre
> Purple palle and armyne fre."

In the "Romaunt of the Rose" the dress of Mirth is described as follows:—

> "Full yong he was, and merry of thought,
> And in samette, with birdes wrought,
> And with gold beten full fetously
> His bodie was clad full richely."
> *   *   *   *   *
>
> "A coronell on hur hedd sett,
> Hur clothys wyth bestes and byrdes wer bete,
> All abowte for pryde."

And now contrast all this with the extreme poverty of the dress of the present day, and turn our thoughts for a moment to those terrible cylindrical enormities the pot-hat and trousers.

Dress? we don't dress—we simply cover our nakedness—as in architecture we are content if we keep out wind and wet. We have forgotten how to dress as we have forgotten how to build, and beauty has forsaken dress as it has forsaken the rest of the decorative arts. Dress is, or should be, one of the decorative arts; the adornment of a "human," assuming that Nature's marvel must be covered, is, to say the very least, as important as the adornment of a brick wall. What is the explanation of the wave of Philistinism which swept not only England but the rest of the world at the beginning of the nineteenth century? Can it be the rise of science, which, bringing in its wake the mechanical fiend, has reduced everything to rule and compass, and thus brought about the death of the æsthetic sense? No other period of the world's history but some country forged ahead and kept alight the sacred lamp of beauty.

*   *   *   *   *   *

Trousers are apparently eternal; they date from the beginning, and will endure, one fears, to the end of sublunary time. Of late there has been a tendency, especially amongst middle-aged and elderly men, to affect the knickerbocker, although whether the æsthetic principle is the mainspring of this tendency, coupled with a natural and pardonable desire to exhibit a well-developed calf, or whether, peradventure, the "too old at twenty" cry is at the bottom of it, is a question which provides food for reflection.

What, then, in view of this eternity of the trouser, can be done to bring it abreast of modern taste and thought? because we *do* move in matters of taste, although almost imperceptibly. Speaking as a designer, it seems only possible to develop the trouser in one of two different directions—that of the peg-top or the bell-bottom. Bell-bottoms may at once be ruled out of the running, since they have become so identified with the coster fraternity that no man of fashion would dream of adopting them. These, then, are the two extremes or opposite poles. There is, however, as the late Mr. Gladstone would have said, a third and middle course—*their columnar character might be retained, and even emphasised*. The shafts might be fluted, as in the Corinthian Order, or festooned, as in the "Prentice pillar."

LONDON PROMENADE DRESS, 1836.

In all seriousness, however, the trouser is an absurdity even from the point of view of mere comfort. A man cannot sit down without first hitching himself up at the knee. The knee is the natural place for the garment to be drawn in, as a certain degree of looseness is necessary at that point in order to allow of the free movement of the limb. Nature herself rebels against the trouser, and does her level best to produce variety of fold, which makes for beauty. Philistine man, however, decides otherwise, and that singular invention the trouser-stretcher—true emblem of the modern spirit of incongruity—is called into play, to undo during the night Nature's doings of the previous day.

The late Lord Salisbury, in his speech at the Royal Academy Banquet on April 30, 1887, is reported as saying: "Then consider the costume of the period. Dresses seem to have been selected by the existing English generation with a special desire to flout and gibe at and repudiate all possibility of compliance with any sense of beauty. I am taxing my memory, but I cannot remember any sculptor who has been bold enough to give a life statue of any English notability in the evening dress of the period. I am quite sure that if that man exists he must be strongly tempted to commit suicide the moment his work appears."

The *Tailor and Cutter*—delightfully fascinating print!—has thrown out many dark hints lately of impending startling changes in men's attire. By the way, *who* are the Rhadamanthine spirits who sit mysteriously in judgment upon these high matters, issuing their fateful decrees, regulating the delicate and subtle curves of the brim of a pot-hat or the turn of a coat collar? Perhaps the *Tailor and Cutter* knows, but, upon the principle that knowledge is power, declines to say; anyway, whatever changes the immediate future may have in store for us, we may take comfort from the fact that they must necessarily be in the direction of betterment, since, having recently emerged from that bottomless pit of all that is æsthetically terrible—the Victorian era: the era of the crinoline, the antimacassar, and of wax flowers under glass—we could not possibly strike a lower depth.

II
THE TUNIC

"Where were the variegated robes, works of Sidonian wom-
en, which god-like Paris himself brought from Sidon, sailing over
the wide sea, along the course by which he conveyed high-born
Helen?" —*Iliad*, vi. 289.

II

THE TUNIC

The earliest made-up garment, that in which the art of the tailor was called into play, was doubtless a simple bag, more or less closely fitting to the body and of varying length, with holes for the arms and an opening for the neck. Such a primitive garment has been worn in varying forms at all periods of the world's history, and is in use at the present time in the form of the ordinary singlet. The modern singlet is, in fact, the simple, primeval type of the tunic.

The coat of many colours which Israel made for his son Joseph was unquestionably an embroidered tunic, although probably made loose and ample. The little coat which the mother of Samuel made for her child when he was dedicated to the priesthood, and brought to him from year to year, was doubtless of the same character.

Sir Henry Layard, describing the dresses of the Assyrians, says "many are represented naked, but the greater number are dressed in short chequered tunics with a long fringe attached to the girdle."

Some remarkable discoveries have been made during the last thirty years in different portions of Scandinavia, which serve to give us a very clear idea of the dress of both men and women of the remote period of the Bronze Age. The dresses were found in coffins made of an oak-tree split in two and hollowed out, the bodies having been buried completely dressed. An illustration is given of a simple woollen tunic with short sleeves and a petticoat with girdle. This was found at Borum, in the neighbourhood of Aarhus, Jutland.

The tunic was worn by the Egyptians. It is seen in their sculptures, paintings, and papyri, and may be said to have formed their principal garment, after the mere loin cloth. The illustrations given are taken from the papyrus of Hunefer, or "Book of the Dead," in the British Museum. The first cut discovers Hunefer, "overseer of the palace of the lord of two lands, Men-maât-Rā (Seti I., King of Egypt about B.C. 1370), and overseer of the cattle of the lord of the two lands, the royal scribe," and his wife Nasha, a lady of the college of the god Amen-Rā at Thebes, in the attitude of adoration.

TUNIC, PETTICOAT AND GIRDLE, BRONZE AGE (JUTLAND).

From "Industrial Arts of Old Denmark" (Worsaae).

Hunefer wears a long tunic with sleeves, ornamented at the throat and neck, with a broad sash around the waist. His wife also wears a long tunic with sleeves, probably tied in with a band underneath the breasts; it is not clear in the drawing. The material is of a light tissue, semi-transparent.

HUNEFER AND HIS WIFE IN ATTITUDE OF ADORATION ("BOOK OF THE DEAD," C. B.C. 1370).

From the Papyrus of Hunefer, or "Book of the Dead," c. B.C. 1370.

The second illustration shows a priest wearing nothing but a loin cloth and a leopard skin.

In the Victoria and Albert Museum is a child's tunic, discovered in a tomb at Alkmîm (Panopolis), Upper Egypt. It is of unbleached linen, dyed blue, with a pattern produced by means of what is called "a reserve," the design being first stamped on the fabric by means of a waxy substance which protected those portions of the dress from the dye into which it was afterwards dipped. The "reserve" was then removed by a second bath, leaving the pattern in the original colour of the fabric.

A PRIEST BURNING INCENSE ("BOOK OF THE DEAD")

From the Papyrus of Hunefer, or "Book of the Dead," c. B.C. 1370.

With the Greeks the tunic was the principal article of attire. It was worn next to the skin, and was of a light tissue. In the earlier time it was composed of wool, in later periods of flax, and in the latest periods it was either of flax mixed with silk or of pure silk. The illustration given will serve to show its construction. It was a simple square bag, open at the two ends, made sufficiently wide to admit of the folds being ample, and sufficiently long to allow of its being gathered up about the waist and breasts. It was kept in its place by various means, either by a simple girdle round the waist or by cords drawn crosswise between the breasts, over the shoulders, looped at the back, and again drawn round the waist, or by an arrangement of cords or ribbons drawn over each shoulder and attached to the girdle.

Over the tunic was a second garment, intended to afford additional protection to the upper part of the body. This was a kind of bib or super-tunic, and was composed of a square or rather oblong piece of stuff, suspended round the chest and back and secured at the shoulders by means of fibulæ or buttons. In some cases the bib was made deeper under the arms, so as to allow the garment to fall in regular zigzag folds, ending in a point, which was weighted with little pellets of lead in order to ensure a better falling of the folds.

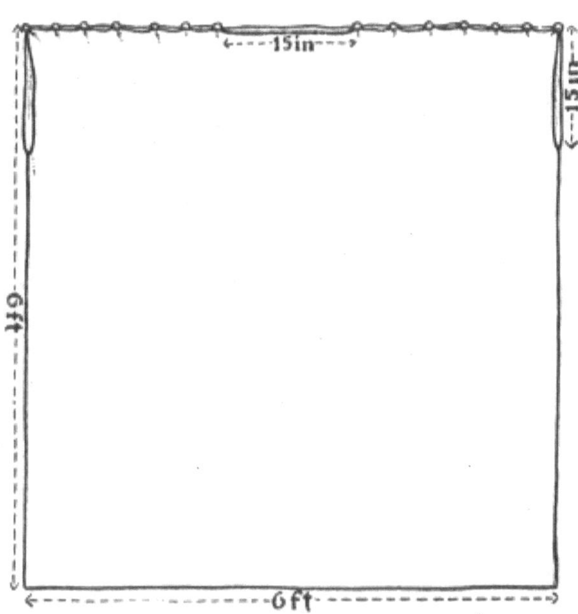

PLAN OF THE TUNIC

The tunic, as well as the super-tunic, was often ornamented with rich borders and diapered with sprigs, spots, stars, &c. The tunic of the Roman women reached to the feet, with the exception of that worn by the Lacedemonian girls, which was short, and also divided at the sides so as to show their thighs; and "this indecency," says Strutt, was countenanced by the laws of Lycurgus.

Horace, in his twenty-fifth Ode, addressing an old woman affecting youth—"flaunting wife of the indigent Ibycus"—exclaims—

"What becomes thee best is a warm woollen dress;
Get thee fleeces from famous Luceria."

Broadly speaking, classic dress consisted of but two elements—the tunic and mantle, both being worn of a thicker material during cold weather. Ulysses exclaims, in the "Odyssey"—

"I have no cloak; the fates have cheated me,
And left alone my tunic."

Dion Cassius has given us an account of the dress of Boadicea, Queen of the Iceni. He says she wore a tunic woven chequerwise in purple, red and blue, and over it a shorter garment open on the bosom. Her yellow hair floated in the wind,

and upon her shoulders was a mantle fastened by a fibula. It was, in fact, a variation of the Roman dress of tunic and mantle or toga. This was the dress which was
common to all nations, both Gaul, Goth, Visigoth, and Vandal, from the Roman
period to the time of Charlemagne, varied, however, according to climatic conditions, and ornamented in the manner peculiar to the particular country.

THE TUNIC (HOPE'S "COSTUME OF THE ANCIENTS").

From Hope's "Costume of the Ancients."

Mr. Planché ("Cyclopædia of Costume") says: "That in this chequered cloth
we see the original *breacan feile*, the garb of old Gaul, still the national dress of the
Scotch Highlanders, there can be no doubt; and that it was at this time the common
habit of every Keltic tribe, though now abandoned by all their descendants except
the hardy and unsophisticated Gaelic mountaineers, is admitted, I believe, by every antiquary who has made public his opinion on the subject."

Eginhart, a writer of the ninth century, has left us a detailed description of the
dress of Charlemagne. It consisted of the following parts: The shirt, the drawers,
the tunic, the stockings, the leg bandages, the shoes, the sword-belt, and sword.
In the winter he added the mantle and the *thorax*, which was, as its name implies,
a covering for the chest and throat. It was made of otter's skin, and was probably
worn underneath the tunic, as no pictured or other representation of this garment
is available.

His tunic was ornamented with a *border of silk*. The material of the tunic itself
is not mentioned, but Strutt thinks that, according to the custom of the time, it was
made of linen. It was the *short* tunic, as the historian positively asserts that he wore
the longer tunic but twice in his life.[6]

[6] With the object of making more complete a work on ancient textile fabrics which
the Prussian Government is issuing, the sarcophagus at Aix-la-Chapelle Cathedral in which

Another French writer quoted by Strutt mentions stockings and *trowsers*, the latter of linen, but ornamented with precious workmanship, *i.e.,* embroidery as forming part of the dress of the Franks.

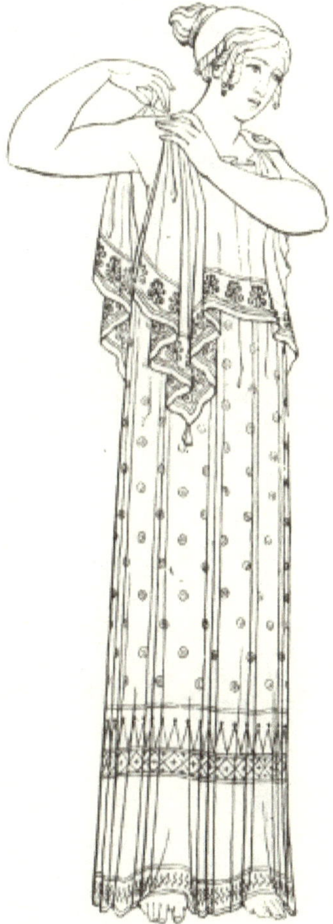

GREEK FIGURE (IBID.).

From Hope's "Costume of the Ancients."

the remains of Charlemagne rest has been opened, and certain pieces of valuable silk have been extracted in order that they may be examined and photographed. The great Frankish Emperor's bones were wrapped in these costly cloths. One of them is ancient Constantinople work, the production of the celebrated Imperial Byzantine workshops, and represents a brilliantly coloured surface with elephants embroidered in circles. The other piece is believed to be of Sicilian origin, with a design of birds and hares.

Charlemagne's bones are still intact, with the exception of the skull and one arm, which are in another part of the Cathedral. Medical men who have examined these bones say that the Emperor was a man of huge proportions. The Kaiser is greatly interested in the preparation of this work on ancient tissues, and it was his Majesty who induced the Archbishop of Cologne to consent to the opening of the sarcophagus.—*Daily Paper.*

Fortunately, we are able to form a very complete idea of Frankish dress from the sculptured effigies of Clovis and his Queen Clothilde on the façade of the Cathedral of Chartres, and other records which have come down to us. The pencil, or the sculptor's chisel, must necessarily be more eloquent and convincing than any written description can possibly be. The general appearance of the Queen may, however, be described as follows: She wears a long loose tunic of soft material, reaching to the ground, confined by a falling girdle with an oval clasp in front, in which emeralds, amethysts and rubies vie with each other in their brilliance. The sleeves are long and ample, the edges serrated in the form of leaves. The long flowing embroidered mantle is fastened by a gold fibula at the throat. Her flaxen hair falls in two long double plaits in front of her person, reaching almost to the ground; the plaits being first bound singly by a dark ribbon, and each pair bound together by a lighter ribbon. A thin gauze veil covers the head, which is surmounted by a crown of exquisite workmanship.

GREEK FIGURE (IBID.).

From Hope's "Costume of the Ancients."

The dress of the Byzantine women, at the time of the dismemberment of the Roman Empire in 395, was still the loose or semi-loose tunic, with sleeves added, elaborately ornamented in the rich diapered patterns peculiar to that period and nation, and confined at the waist by a girdle. This costume, with variations, obtained until the Norman Conquest, when costume began to be more complex. The long loose gown is variously described in documents of the period by the names of the tunic, the *gunna* or gown, and the kirtle. There was a short tunic, with sleeves reaching only to the elbows, and there was a long tunic, with tight sleeves, worn underneath. The kirtle, such as we are familiarised with in the dress of a later period, had not come into being. As a matter of fact, the term "kirtle" is indiscriminately used in the description of various garments. Tyrwhitt describes it as "a tunic or waistcoat."

In the "Romaunt of the Rose" the "damoselles right young" are arrayed—

> "In kirtles and noon other wede,"

evidently here intended for a long gown or tunic.

The dress of the twenty young squires chosen by Guy of Warwick is thus described:—

> "Kyrtyls they had oon of sylke
> Also whyte, as any mylke.
> Of gode sylke and of purpull palle
> Mantels above they caste all.
> Hosys they had uppon, but no schone;
> Barefote they were everychone."

Both Strutt and some other writers on the subject of costume appear to be puzzled by the *colouring* of the earlier illuminators, principally, however, with respect to the colour of the hair and beard, but also in regard to the various details of costume. They remark the curious circumstance of the hair and beard being painted *blue*. "In representations of old men this might be considered only to indicate *grey hair*; but even the flowing locks of Eve are painted blue in one MS., and the heads of youth and age exhibit the same cerulean tint." Strutt argues from this that some art of tinting or dyeing was practised. A writer who quotes Strutt says: "The hair being painted sometimes *green* and *orange* is in favour of this argument, but such instances are very rare, and may have arisen from the idleness of the illuminator, who daubed it, perhaps, with the nearest colour at hand." This, however, was not in the least so. The explanation is, as any *educated* artist knows (artists are not *all* educated), that with the old illuminator *the decoration of the page* was his first consideration—rightly so; and the colour of the hair and beard, together with the precise tint of the gown, would incline to either blue, red, or yellow, accordingly as the exigencies of the general colour scheme demanded. This fact should always be kept in mind in considering the colour of any illuminated MS.

This colouring is amusingly parodied by Mr. Punch in his book of British costumes (1860). He gives a fragment of a love song, "commonly believed to have been written by King Vortigern, who was inveigled into marriage with the daughter of old Hengist":—

"Rowena is my ladye-love,
Her robe itte is a gunna;
Shee wears blewe haire her ears above,
O is shee notte a stunna!"

He adds: "Critics disagree as to the meaning of the word 'stunna,' but we incline, ourselves, to think it was a bit of Saxon slang, and from the context we imagine it was used by way of compliment."

**"TREUTHE'S PILGRYME ATTE PLOW
(TRINITY COLLEGE, CAMBRIDGE)."**

From the MS. R. 3, 14 in the Library of Trinity College, Cambridge.

A development of the super-tunic was the surcoat, which was worn by either sex during the thirteenth and fourteenth centuries. It assumed a variety of forms, and was either a long loose outer garment, variously shaped and sleeveless, or, as during the reign of Richard II., was a shorter, closely-fitting jacket or coat with sleeves, and usually trimmed with miniver or other fur.

The surcoat, or super-tunic, during the Anglo-Saxon period, was worn by the nobility only, and was therefore made of the most costly material, of silk or of finest linen, and often richly embroidered. As a matter of fact, embroidery always forms a conspicuous element in Anglo-Saxon dress, the Anglo-Saxon women being famous for their skill with the needle. We learn from Eginhart that the four Princesses, daughters of Edward the Elder, and sisters to Æthelstan, were celebrated for their skill in spinning, weaving, and embroidering, and Editha, the wife of Edward the Confessor, was a perfect mistress of the needle.

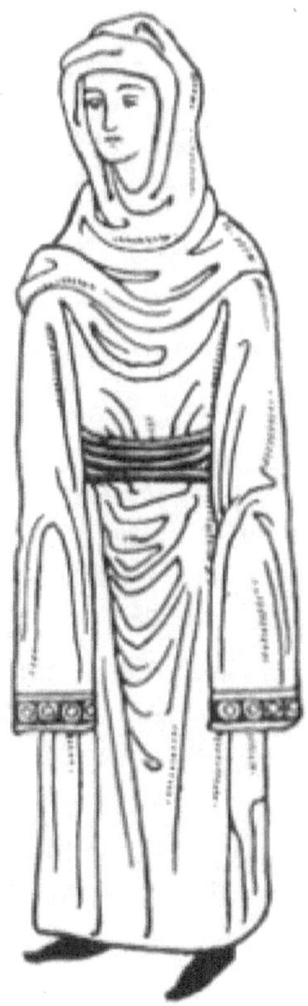

ANGLO-SAXON DRESS (EIGHTH CENTURY).

A somewhat remarkable feature of Anglo-Saxon dress of the eighth century was the long super-tunic with long sleeves, worn in travelling or during cold weather. The sleeves not only cover the hands, but reach considerably below the tips of the fingers. The sleeves worn by the Chinese mandarins at the present time are identical with the long sleeves of the Anglo-Saxon period.

The tunic, so far as women's dress is concerned, may be said to have finally disappeared by the time of the Tudors, when a woman's dress consisted of kirtle or petticoat, and bodice or stomacher. Indeed, the tunic proper may be said to have disappeared with the general change which came about in costume immediately after the Norman Conquest, the Saxon word "gunna" and the Norman "surcoat" better describing the dresses of that period.

The term "tunic" is also applied to the military surcoat of the present time, this article of military costume, however, bearing no sort of affinity to the original tunic.

An important adjunct of the tunic was the girdle, by which the garment was looped up and confined within reasonable limits. In the case of the men, as Strutt observes, it served a double purpose, that of confining the tunic, and supporting the sword.

Girdles were of various kinds—a sash of silk or other materials; or formed of leather, either a simple thong or ornamented in various ways; or of different cloths, richly embroidered and studded with jewels; or of metal. The girdle of Charlemagne was composed of gold and silver.

> "A girdel ful riche for the nanes
> Of perry and of precious stanes."

> *Ywaine and Gawin.*

The Imperial girdle of the Holy Roman Empire was woven in silk and gold, having a woven inscription upon the narrow border, and clasped by means of a heavy gilt buckle.

It is recorded that upon the return of Henry VI. to England after his coronation in France in 1432 the Lord Mayor of London rode to meet him at Eltham, "being arrayed in crimson velvet, a great velvet hat furred, a girdle of gold about his middle, and a baldrick of gold about his neck trailing down behind him."

Numerous fine examples of the girdle occur among the early brasses. It was used also by both sexes for the purpose of suspending or sustaining the pouch or purse which was invariably worn during the Middle Ages, as it was the only form of pocket—

> "And by his gurdil hyng a purs of lethir,
> Tassid with silk, and perled with latoun."

> *Miller's Tale.*

The name "cut-purse" applied to thieves is derived from the circumstance of the leather thongs which attached the pouch to the girdle being slit with a knife.

*   *   *   *   *

Some few years ago a movement, having its origin, singularly enough, in the United States, above all places, was instituted for the purpose of inducing the modern Greeks to adopt the ancient costume of their forefathers, several prominent Americans masquerading in the streets of Athens in tunic and peplum. The only result of the movement was to create a diversion amongst the inhabitants, who probably regarded their would-be instructors as harmless lunatics. The result was, indeed, inevitable; such sentimental movements are predestined to failure. A national costume is of slow growth; it is the natural outcome of the general habits, mode of thought, and temper of a people. It is as impossible to bring about a sudden change in dress as it is to create a new style of architecture.

*   *   *   *   *

At the annual congress of Prussian female elementary school teachers held recently at Altona, some interesting papers were read which are germane to this subject of costume, and which serve to show that some of the continental peoples are more alive to the importance of this subject than we are. We give a short *résumé* which appeared in the pages of the *Daily Chronicle* a short while ago. The italics are ours.

"School-Inspector Muller urged the necessity of reform of children's clothes, stating *that the human body is a most magnificent work of art which is frequently maltreated with corsets and other tightly fitting garments.*

"Fraulein Lischnevska, of Spandau, said a return must be made to the pure art of the ancient Greeks. During gymnastic exercises children must be naked, and only immoral persons would regard this as immoral. This remark was greeted with a storm of applause.

"Fraulein Bertha Jordan, of Mulhausen, *deplored the fact of people becoming so greatly estranged from art, a circumstance which she ascribed to the degradation of work and the severance from nature, both resulting from industrialism.* The remedy, she considers, lies with schools and school education, and she argued that much can be done by a careful selection of pictures on the class-room walls, by awakening faculties of observation in children and arousing their interest in nature which surrounds them."

III
THE MANTLE

The gret Emetreus the Kyng of Ynde
Uppon a steede bay trapped in steel
Covered with cloth and of gold dyapred wel
Cam rydyng lyk the god of armes mars
His coote armour was a cloth of Tars
Cowched of perlys whyte round and grete
His sadil was of brend gold newe bete
A mantelet upon his schuldre hangyng
Bret-ful of Rubies reed and fir sparclyng
His crispe her lik rynges was i-ronne
And that was yalwe and gliteryng as the sonne.

CHAUCER, The Knight's Tale.

HEADING: THE CORONATION MANTLE AT VIENNA.

Preserved in the Imperial Treasury in Vienna.

III

THE MANTLE

Of the famous mantles recorded in history, one of the first which will occur to the mind is that of Elijah, in which he hid his face when he stood in the cave at Horeb, and heard the still, small voice, which came after the fire, which came after the earthquake, which came after the great strong wind which rent the mountains, and brake in pieces the rocks before the Lord. And afterwards, when he "found Elisha the son of Shaphat who was plowing with twelve yoke of oxen before him, and he with the twelfth, Elijah passed by him and *cast his mantle upon him.*"

And again, on the shores of Jordan, "Elijah took his mantle, and wrapped it together, and smote the waters, and they were divided hither and thither, so that they two went over on dry ground."

*   *   *   *   *

"And it came to pass as they still went on, and talked, that, behold, there appeared a chariot of fire, and horses of fire, and parted them both asunder; and Elijah went up by a whirlwind into heaven."

"And Elisha saw it, and he cried, My father, my father, the chariot of Israel, and the horsemen thereof. And he saw him no more; and he took hold of his own clothes, and rent them in two pieces."

"He took up also the mantle of Elijah that fell from him, and went back, and stood by the bank of Jordan."

*   *   *   *   *

"And when the sons of the prophets which were to view at Jericho saw him, they said, The spirit of Elijah doth rest on Elisha. And they came to meet him, and bowed themselves to the ground before him."

St. Martin, Bishop of Tours, soldier of God, dividing his mantle with the beggar at the gates of Amiens, is one of many similar stories in the earlier history of the Christian Church. It is a variation of the story of St. Christopher, and is intended as a lesson in charity. The legend recounts that Christ appeared to him the following night covered with the half of his mantle.

What schoolboy but does not remember the story of Raleigh's mantle, which he cast into the mire in order that Queen Elizabeth's feet might not be soiled? "The night had been rainy, and just where the young gentleman stood, a small quantity of mud interrupted the Queen's passage. As she hesitated to pass on, the gallant, throwing his cloak from his shoulders, laid it on the miry spot, so as to ensure her stepping over it dryshod. Elizabeth looked at the young man, who accompanied this act of devoted courtesy with a profound reverence, and a blush that overspread his whole countenance. The Queen was confused, and blushed in her turn, nodded her head, hastily passed on, and embarked in her barge without saying a word."[7]

The mantle is the cloak or outermost covering to the body, and was originally worn either when the weather was unpropitious, or, as occasion demanded.

The peplum of the Greeks was, in fact, a mantle, worn by both sexes, and was occasionally very long, passing twice round the body, first underneath the arms and then over the shoulder. In rainy or cold weather it was pulled over the head, and also in times of mourning.

The peplum had no clasps or fastenings of any sort, but was kept in its place by its own involutions, of which the combinations were almost endless.

It will readily be understood that the natural foldings of drapery, possessing in themselves so much variety and interest, when thrown over a form so beautifully proportioned as is the human figure, gave the utmost grace of line and form, and this fact makes it all the more surprising that the natural foldings of drapery are not taken greater advantage of in modern dress. The peplum was often diapered with sprigs, spots, stars, or other patternings, and was occasionally richly bordered.

The Greeks also occasionally wore a shorter and simpler cloak, called chlamys, in lieu of the more ample peplum; such a short mantle is the one which we see upon the shoulders of the Apollo Belvidere.

---

[7] Scott's "Kenilworth."

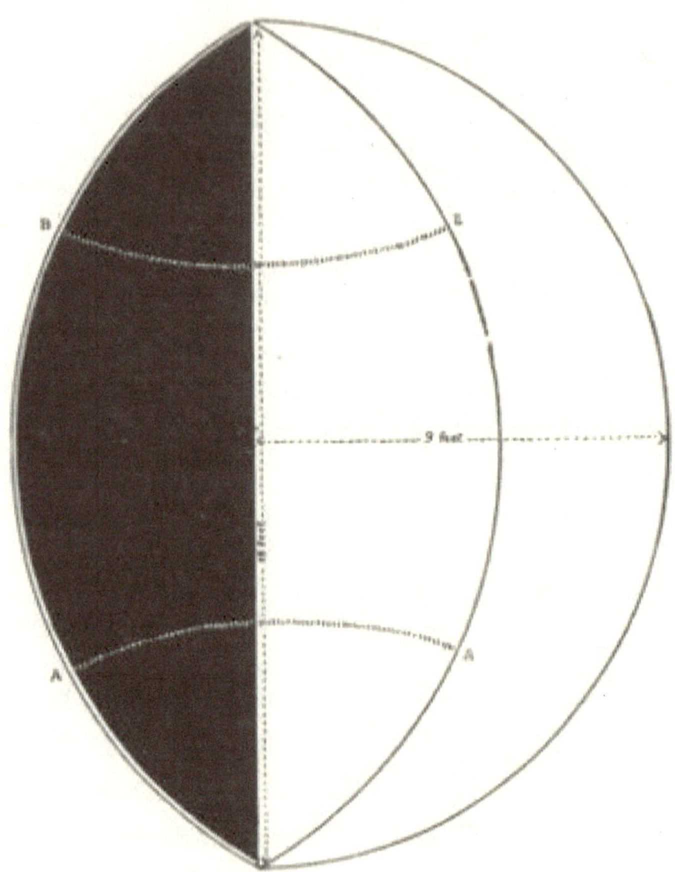

PLAN OF THE TOGA.

The Roman toga corresponded to the Greek peplum, but differed from it in shape, and was more ample, for while the peplum was square, or rather oblong, the toga assumed the form of two semicircles—a larger and a smaller one, or, more correctly speaking, a semicircle and the smaller segment of a circle, which was doubled over the semicircle before adjustment. One end of the toga was then placed upon the left shoulder in such a position that the end or point just touched the ground, the rest of the garment drawn round the back of the figure, underneath the right arm, and flung again over the left shoulder; a sort of loop or bag was then drawn out at the waist in front and served as a pocket. The toga measured 18 feet from tip to tip, or three times the height of a man. It was worn always over the tunic—at any rate during the later Roman time. Horace, in his fourth Epode, thus satirises an upstart:—

> "Mark, as along the Sacred Way thou flauntest,
> Puffing thy toga, twice three cubits wide."

THE TOGA (HOPE'S "COSTUME OF THE ANCIENTS").

From Hope's "Costume of the Ancients."

The material of the toga was wool, in the earlier time and for the common people; afterwards silk and other materials were used, coloured or bordered according to the rank or station of the wearer.

The mantle—that is, the simple square or oblong cloak which was derived from the Greek peplum—was worn in different ways from the Roman period onwards, either thrown loosely over the shoulders as was the peplum, or fastened at the shoulder or breast by means of fibulæ, rings, or cords. In a bas-relief found at Autun and engraved in Montfaucon, an archdruid is represented with a long mantle reaching to the ground, the ends drawn through a ring upon the left shoulder.

The large coronation mantle of the Holy Roman Empire, preserved in the Imperial Treasury at Vienna, is semicircular in shape, of red silk, richly embroidered in gold thread, the outlines emphasised by rows of seed pearls. The design, which is divided in the middle by a representation of a palm tree, figures on either side a lion springing upon a camel, and is treated with that noble convention characteristic of early Sicilian design. On the border of the curved edge is worked an Arabic inscription (common in earlier Sicilian fabrics), stating that the robe was worked in the Royal factory at Palermo in 1134.

One of the gifts which the five maidens present to Beryn from Duke Isope is a purple mantle—

> "The thirde had a mantell of lusty fressh coloure
> The uttir part of purpell i-furred with peloure."

The Tale of Beryn.

The mantle was a distinguishing feature of the costume of the Franks, which was a variation of Roman or classic dress, *i.e.*, the loose tunic and mantle, with the addition of hose or leg covering with cross gartering; both tunic and mantle were often elaborately bordered in a style of ornament which strongly betrayed, in fact, was a development of, Byzantine influences.

King John of Gascogny having been counselled by his barons to yield up to Charlemagne the four sons of Aymon, after much sorrow, summons his secretary—"Come forth, syre Peter, and write a letter from me to the Kinge Charlemagne, as I shall telle you: It is that I sende hym salutacyon wyth goode love, and yf he wyll leve me my londe in peas, I promyse hym that afore ten dayes ben paste, I shall delyver unto hym the foure sones of Aymon, and he shall fynde theym in the playne of Valcolours clothed with scarlette furred wyth ermynes, and ridynge upon mewles, berynge in theyr handes flowres and roses for a token, bycause that men shall better knowe them."

Charlemagne calls then his chamberlain—"Make a lettre to Kyng Yon of Gascoyne in my behalve. Wryte that I sende hym salutacyon and goode love, and that yf he dooth for me as he sayth, I shall encrease his royame wyth fourtene goode castelles, and therof I gyve hym for surete our lorde and saynte Denys of Fraunce, and that I sende hym four mauntelles of scarlette furred wyth ermynes, for to clothe wythall the traytoures, when they shall goo to the playne of Valcoloures, and there they shall be hanged, yf God wyll."[8]

The Venetian mantle which Charlemagne wore was, according to an early French writer quoted by Strutt, of a grey or blue colour. It was quadrangular in its form, and so doubled that when placed upon the shoulders it hung down as low as the feet before and behind, but on the sides it scarcely reached to the knees.

In the Anglo-Saxon dress of the earlier period, the mantle is a simple square with a border on the outer side, the two upper corners being gathered together at the shoulders and fastened with brooches connected by a chain. It is an instance of a very decorative effect being produced by simple means.

---

[8] "The Four Sons of Aymon," Caxton's version.

The coronation mantle of Edward the Confessor was richly embroidered by his Queen, Editha.

William of Malmesbury mentions a mantle presented to Henry I. by Robert Bloet, Bishop of Lincoln, which was lined with black sables with white spots, and cost £100, a large sum in those days.

STATUE OF QUEEN MATILDA AT ROCHESTER.

The mantle, during the Norman period, underwent little change. It was fastened, either upon one of the shoulders, generally the right, or in front, by means of fibulæ or pins of an ornamental character. In the earliest sculptured effigies of English Sovereigns which we possess, those of Henry I. and his Queen Matilda at the west door of Rochester Cathedral, the King is represented in a long dalmatic, with a loose mantle thrown over his left arm. The Queen has a more formal mantle, resting upon either shoulder, the system of fastening of which is hidden by the two long plaits of hair which fall down on either side, but which was probably some kind of ornamental strap. The ordinary mantles of this period were often provided with a "capa" or cowl, which was drawn over the head and frequently used in lieu of a hat.

In the effigies of the Plantagenet Kings, the mantles are generally of the long flowing character above described, varied by rich borderings or embroiderings. Henry II., however, introduced a shorter mantle (cloak of Anjou), from which circumstance he obtained the sobriquet of "Curt manteau." The effigy of Eleanor of Castile, his Queen, in the Abbey of Fontevraud in Normandy, shows a mantle embroidered with a "powdering" of gold crescents. That of Cœur de Lion, in the same Abbey, has a square-bordered mantle fastened at the breast by a fibula at the upper corners. The two lower corners are plainly shown in the statue folded over each other.

During the reign of Henry III. costume generally increased in splendour. The effigy of this monarch, however, exhibits a loose plain mantle, fastened by a fibula on the right shoulder, the folds of the mantle hanging in a series of regular festoons over the front of the figure.

In the Harleian MSS. is a satirical Latin "Song upon the Tailors" of this reign (Henry III.), an English version of which is included in Mr. Wright's "Political Songs," published by the Camden Society. Addressing the tailors, it commences:—

"I have said ye are gods; why should I omit the service which should be said on festival days? Gods certainly ye are, who can transform an old garment into the shape of a new one. The cloth, while fresh and new, is made either a cape or mantle; but, in order of time, first it is a cape, after a little space this is transformed into the other: Thus ye change bodies. When it becomes old, the collar is cut off; when deprived of the collar it is made a mantle: Thus in the manner of Proteus are garments changed. When at length winter returns, many engraft immediately upon the cape a capuce; then it is squared; after being squared it is rounded, and so it becomes an amice. If there remain any morsels of the cloth or skin which is cut, they do not want a use: of these are made gloves. This is the general manner, they all make one robe out of another, English, Germans, French, and Normans, with scarcely an exception. Thus *cape* is declined, but *mantel* otherwise: in the first year while it is fresh, the skin and the cloth being both new, it is laid up in a box; when, however, the fur begins to be worn off, and the thread of the seams broken, the fur is clipped and placed on a new mantle, until at last, in order that nothing may be lost, it is given to the servant for his wages."

LORD BURLEIGH, 1520-1598. (NATIONAL PORTRAIT GALLERY).

Photo by Emery Walker.

The vestments of the most noble Order of the Garter, founded, as every student of history knows, in the reign of Edward III.,[9] consisted originally of a mantle, a tunic, and capuchon, of blue woollen cloth, cut to the fashion of the period, the knights differing only from the monarchs in respect of the tunic being lined with miniver instead of ermine. All three garments were closely diapered or powdered with garters of gold, the mantle having one larger than the rest on the left shoulder, enclosing a shield, Argent, with the cross of St. George, Gules.

The vestments of this Order have been constantly altered during different periods. In the seventh year of Richard II. the surcoat or tunic was of "violet in grain," in the eleventh year white, and in the twelfth and nineteenth of "long blue cloth." They were changed again to white in the first year of Henry V., another change to scarlet in the reign of Henry VI., and afterwards back again to white.

[9] This chivalrous monarch not only founded the Order of the Garter, but even contemplated the revival of the Round Table.

The number of embroidered garters on the coat and chaperon were in this reign limited to 120 for a duke, 110 for a marquis, 90 for an earl, decreasing in the same ratio to 60 in the case of a knight bachelor. The King's was unlimited; on the surcoat and hood of Henry VI. there were 173.

The material of the mantle was changed to velvet during this reign, lined with white damask or satin.

In the reign of Henry VII. an important addition was made to the insignia of this Order, that of the *collar*. The whole habit sent to the King of Castile in the twenty-seventh year of this reign consisted of mantle, kirtle, hood and *collar*, and was of purple velvet lined with silk or sarcenet, the embroidered garters entirely disappearing.

The Statutes of the Order were reformed by Henry VIII., who also altered the dress to the fashion of the period. The flat velvet hat or cap, so familiar in Holbein's portraits, superseded the chaperon or hood, which was, however, still worn hung or depending upon the shoulder, and called the *humerale*. Both hat and surcoat were of crimson velvet.

The lesser *George*, or jewel of the Order, was introduced during this reign, suspended upon the breast by either a gold chain or riband, which latter was *black*.

In the reign of Elizabeth, the flat hat gives place to one with a higher crown, being more in keeping with the fashion of the time, but no other alteration of the habit was made.

During the reign of Charles II. ostrich or heron plumes appear in the cap, and the broad blue riband was worn over the left shoulder and under the right arm.

As at present worn, the mantle is of purple velvet lined with taffetas, bearing on the left shoulder the badge of the Order, viz., a silver escutcheon charged with the red cross of St. George and enriched with the garter and motto. In chapters it is worn over the uniform or Court dress. The surcoat, or short gown without sleeves, is made of crimson velvet, lined, like the mantle, with white taffetas silk. The hood, worn on the right shoulder of the mantle, is made of the same velvet as the surcoat, and lined with the same material.

Matthew Paris, describing the solemnisation of the marriage of Alexander III. of Scotland with the Princess Margaret, sister of Henry III., says:—

"There were great abundance of people of all ranks, multitudes of the nobility of England, France, and Scotland, with crowds of Knights and military Officers, the whole of them pompously adorned with garments of silk, and so transformed with excess of Ornaments that it would be impossible to describe their dresses without being tiresome to the reader, though it would excite his astonishment. Upwards of one thousand Knights on the part of the King of England attended the nuptials in vestments of silk, curiously wrought in embroidery; and these vestments on the morrow were laid aside; and the same Knights appeared in new robes of still more magnificent decoration. The nobles of Scotland and of France did not fall a whit below those of England in their show and parade. The Barons and the Knights were habited in robes of divers colours; sometimes they appeared

in green, sometimes in blue, then again in grey, and afterwards in scarlet, varying the colours according to their fancies, or the wills of the ladies to whom they
had dedicated their amorous vows. Their breasts were adorned with fibulæ, or
brooches of gold; and their shoulders with precious stones of great magnitude,
such as emeralds, sapphires, jacinths, pearls, rubies, and other rich ornaments. The
ladies who attended had rings of gold, set with topaz stones and diamonds, upon
their fingers; their heads were adorned with elegant crests or garlands; and their
wimples were composed of the richest stuffs, embroidered with pure gold, and
embellished with the rarest jewellery."

LODOWICK, DUKE OF RICHMOND AND LENNOX.

Engraved by J. Barrà.

In an inventory of the wardrobe and jewels of Henry V., taken in 1423 at his decease, mention is made of *heukes* of scarlet cloth and camlet, and *pilches* of grey fur. The word *pilche* is a corruption of the Latin *pelliceus*, or the Saxon *pylce*, and represented a coat of fur worn during cold weather. The modern word *pelisse* used to describe a child's coat is derived from the same source.[10]

"After grete hete comith colde,
No man cast his pilche away."

CHAUCER.

**PORTION OF THE PICTURE OF THE MIRACLE
OF ST. BERNARD PERUGIA.**

By Fiorenzo di Lorenzo, Pinacoteca, Perugia.

[10] Pilch or pilcher, a scabbard, a *covering* for the sword.

A farewell letter of Bishop Ridley (Foxe's "Book of Martyrs"), describing the sufferings of Christ's true soldiers, says:—

"They were stoned, hewn asunder, tempted, fell, and were slain upon the edge of the sword; some wandered to and fro in sheep's pilches, in goats' pilches, forsaken, oppressed, afflicted."

In the inventory above referred to are mentioned, "gounes de noier damask, furrez de sides de foynes et marterons." The cost of these furs is also given—"iii pares de foyns, chascun cont' c. bestes, pris le pec' x*d.* xii*li.* xs.," the marteron being more costly.

The foyne appears to have been the same as the polecat or fitchet.

The pylce was in common use during the Anglo-Saxon period, and worn by all classes. In Michel's "Chroniques Anglo-Normandes," *c.* 1185, is described a meeting on a little bridge near Westminster between Tosti, Earl of Huntingdon, and Siward, Earl of Northumberland. "The said Earl approached so near to Siward on the bridge that he dirtied his pelisse (*pelles*) with his miry feet; for it was then customary for noblemen to use skins without cloth." This evidently referring to a long mantle or cloak.

The Anglo-Saxon Chronicle mentions the great gifts and many treasures of skins decked with purple, pelisses of marten skin, weasel skin, and ermine skin, which King Malcolm of Scotland and his sister Margaret gave to the Conqueror in 1074.

During the general change which came about in costume in the reign of Richard II. a shorter mantle or cloak began to be worn, which continued at intervals and under various forms until the universal adoption of coats at the close of the reign of Charles II.

In the tempera painting of the miracle of St. Bernard by Fiorenzo di Lorenzo in the Pinacoteca at Perugia, a young man is wearing a short cloak or mantle, hanging in very formal folds from the shoulder and reaching a little below the middle. The mantle is buttoned upon the right shoulder, thus repeating the principle of the Roman toga, which leaves the right arm free. A similar short cloak is figured in a copy of Froissart's Chronicles in the Harleian MSS. in the British Museum. There was a reason for the mantle being fastened upon the right shoulder; it was that the right arm is the sword-arm. This, however, does not apply to the toga, which is the last garment that a man would fight in. Two other figures in the picture above mentioned are habited in long cloaks reaching to the feet, with full sleeves; the cloak of the dark figure lined and bordered with miniver, and the other of a different fur.

These long robes with ample sleeves constantly occur in Benozzo Gozzoli's frescoes in the Campo Santo at Pisa, either flowing loosely or confined by a girdle, and generally lined and bordered with miniver, which appears to be a favourite enrichment with Benozzo. These garments are worn usually by more elderly persons.

In a small but extremely elaborate and beautiful picture by Fra Angelico, in the

Convent of San Marco at Florence, a figure appears habited in one of these long robes, having openings for the sleeves of the under garment, which are of a different material, to pass through. The dress is confined by a rich girdle.

During the reign of Elizabeth the short cloak, or cape cloak, continued to be worn. It reached scarcely below the waistbelt, was provided with a collar, which was often deep, and was lined with silk or satin of a different colour to the outside, often extremely rich.

> "Here is a cloke cost fifty pound, wife,
> Which I can sell for thirty when I have seen
> All London in't, and London has seen me."

BEN JONSON, The Devil is an Ass.

The Spanish cloak was thrown loosely over the shoulders somewhat after the manner of the toga. It was customary to wrap it around the left arm to serve as a shield in duels.

In the portrait of Prince Henry, eldest son of James I. (p. 103), the Prince is figured as wearing a long mantle reaching to the knees. It has a collar, a richly jewelled border, and is lined with silk damask.

The Puritan cloak did not differ materially in shape from that worn by the Cavaliers, but, like the rest of Puritan dress, was entirely bare of ornament: —

"He was tall and fair, and had plain but very good cloaths on his back" (Bunyan, "Life of Mr. Badman").

There are a number of references to dress in Pepys's "Diary," which covers a period of ten years, 1659-69.

Under date July 1, 1660, he writes: "This morning came home my fine camlett cloak, with gold buttons, and a silk suit, which cost me much money, and I pray God to make me able to pay for it."

About this time a shorter cloak, reaching to a little below the waist, came into fashion. On October 7th (Lord's Day) of the same year, 1660, occurs the entry: "To Whitehall on foot, calling at my father's to change my long black cloake for a short one, (long cloakes being now quite out), but he being gone to church, I could not get one."

Under date October 22, 1663, occurs an entry which refers to the *material* of the cloak. The Queen was ill of the spotted fever, and, upon hearing that she had grown worse, he sends to his tailor to stop the making of his velvet cloak (presumably coloured) "till I see whether she lives or dies."

The velvet, however, referred to the lining of the cloak, which was often richer than the outside. On the 29th of the following month (the Queen had recovered and was about again) he dons his best black cloth suit, trimmed with scarlet ribbon, very neat, and his "cloak lined with velvet, and a new beaver, which altogether is very noble."

PRINCE HENRY, ELDEST SON OF JAMES I.

In the reign of William III. the long skirted coats of the men, with waistcoats reaching to the knees, rendered any outer clothing unnecessary, except for the coldest weather, when long cloaks were worn, together with muffs, by the beaux.

Muffs were at this period worn as commonly by men as by women, and this fashion continued for nearly a century.

The beau with his muff is thus satirised in the comic opera "Lionel and Clarissa," by Isaac Bickerstaff, *c.* 1768:—

> "A coxcomb, a fop, a dainty milk-sop;
> Who, essenc'd and dizen'd from bottom to top,
> Looks just like a doll for a milliner's shop.
> A thing full of prate, and pride and conceit;
> All fashion, no weight;
> Who shrugs and takes snuff; and carries a muff;
> A minnikin, finicking, French powder-puff!"

EARL OF ROCHESTER, 1641-1711. (NATIONAL PORTRAIT GALLERY).

Kneller, National Portrait Gallery.

Photo by Walker & Cockerell.

The mantle does not appear to have particularly excited the wrath of the satirists. It is, indeed, so entirely reasonable a garment both for men and women, that it is difficult to see how it could possibly provide material for satire.

Broadly speaking, there are three conditions necessary to beautiful dress, namely, beauty of material, excellence of workmanship, and variety of fold. If ornament be introduced, it should be of a good character, and employed rather in accordance with those well understood laws of contrast than an indiscriminate covering of the whole field; in fact, this defeats its own purpose, as richness of effect depends upon concentration, as a painter focusses light, colour, or other interest in a particular part of his work and allows nothing to detract from it. As a general rule, plain spaces are best adapted for ornamentation, although in the rich brocades of the fine periods the foldings of the material give an added richness and variety to the patterning.

The mantle, therefore, is usually bare of ornament or simply bordered, except for occasions of high ceremony; certainly plain if worn loosely, and many foldings ensue; and any richness of ornament is confined to the more closely fitting portions of the dress. In a word, the decorative conditions of dress are as well defined, as absolute, as in any other of the ornamental arts.

DUKE OF BUCKINGHAM.

IV
THE DOUBLET AND HOSE

"Monsieur, the King's elder brother, has set up for a kind of wit; and leans towards the Philosophe side. Monseigneur d'Artois pulls the mask from a fair impertinent; fights a duel in consequence,—almost drawing blood. He has breeches of a kind new in this world;—a fabulous kind, 'four tall lackeys,' says Mercier, as if he had seen it, 'hold him in the air, that he may fall into the garment without vestige of wrinkle; from which rigorous encasement the same four, in the same way, and with more effort, have to deliver him at night.'"—CARLYLE, *French Revolution*, Book II., Chap. I.

South Kensington Museum.

IV

THE DOUBLET AND HOSE

The absence of wrinkle or fold, alluded to in the above quotation, is commonly suggestive of the modern spirit in dress. The first thing an artist does in painting a figure in hose is to indicate the little wrinkles or folds at the knee and ankle. This, as serving two purposes, first as a decorative enrichment to the limb, and secondly as indicating, together with the colour of the material, the fact that the limb is clothed. There are, however, such things as "fleshings," which are made of some material possessing elasticity, and so reducing the wrinkles and folds to a minimum; but if there is one thing more than another which is characteristic of clothing or drapery, it is its *folds*—their constant and endless change varying with every movement. The ideal of modern tailoring appears to be something which shall have as near as possible the appearance of a deal board, to eliminate as far as possible the foldings of drapery with their infinite variety and almost endless play of light and shade.

With the doublet and hose we deal with a comparatively recent period, when dress generally assumed a more formal character, and the loose tunic gave place to the more closely fitting doublet.

Long before this, however, the sleeves had developed in various ways, in strange and fantastic shapes. In the reign of Richard II.—

> "Cut worke was great both in Court and townes,
> Bothe in men's hoodes and also in their gownes,
> Broudur[11] and furre and goldsmith's worke all newe
> In many a wyse each day they did renewe."
>
> HARDING'S *Chronicle.*

The tight sleeves of the reigns of the three Edwards had given place to a sleeve

---

[11] Embroidery.

of more ample proportions. The monk of Evesham speaks of "pokys" shaped like a bagpipe: "The devil's receptacles, for whatever was stolen could be popped into them."

The "cut work" above alluded to was extremely fantastic, the jagged edgings of the sleeves, and, indeed, the rest of the costume, taking the shape of the serrations of leaves, as well as other ornamental devices.

In the reign of Edward IV. the short jackets, doublets, or pourpoints, were provided with closely fitting sleeves, which were divided at the elbow and shoulder, allowing the shirt or under-garment to appear as puffing, tied with ribbons at these points, and laced underneath up the whole length of the arm.

**FIGURE FROM THE MIRACLE OF ST. BERNARD
BY FIORENZO DI LORENZO, PERUGIA.**

By Fiorenzo di Lorenzo, Pinacoteca, Perugia.

Another development of the sleeve, which lasted for a long period, was the addition of an outer sleeve with a slit in the middle to allow of the arm with its tight sleeve being passed through, the rest of the sleeve hanging down. This was ornamented in a variety of ways, either by edgings of fur or by embroidery.

Hose, that is, the more or less tightly fitting nether garments, be they breche, hosen, or what not, have been worn from a very early period. An illustration is given, from Hope's "Costume of the Ancients," of Paris on Mount Ida, in which he is figured as wearing a closely fitting garment which covers the whole body and limbs, being buttoned all the way up the legs and arms; a short tunic, also buttoned up the front, being worn over this dress. A similar tightly fitting dress was, in fact, worn by the Amazonian women.

The cross-gartering, worn by the Goths, Franks, Anglo-Saxons, and other nations, is referred to under the "shoe," of which it usually formed a part. Some kind of hose, stockings, or bandages was invariably worn underneath the gartering, which often extended the whole length of the leg. This cross-gartering probably originated with the practice among the peasants of enswathing the legs with hay-bands.

The short trouser of the Normans, or tunic and trouser in one, with short sleeves attached, of which so many examples occur in the Bayeux tapestry, is a garment which has puzzled many writers, on account of the apparent difficulty of putting it on. It appears to have been put on from below upwards, by being drawn on the thighs, and afterwards putting the arms in the sleeves. In the illustration given of a similar dress (p. 116), the metal plates or pieces of leather which serve as armour are added to the front of the dress only. The cross-gartering in this instance would probably not reach above the knees.

From the Norman period onwards, tight hose continued to be worn, and presented little variation except in the matter of colour and material. The parti-coloured hose of the Plantagenet period and later called forth many strictures from the satirists and moralists, chiefly clerical, of the time. "The red side of a gentleman, they declared, gave them the idea of his having been half roasted, or that he and his dress were afflicted by *St. Anthony's fire!*"[12]

---

[12] Fairholt, "Costume in England."

PARIS ON MOUNT IDA (HOPE'S "COSTUME OF THE ANCIENTS").

From Hope's "Costume of the Ancients."

This parti-colouring presented many variations. The legs were either plain, dark and light alternately, of various colours, black and red, black and yellow; or a variation of one colour, red, yellow, or grey, as the case may be; or one leg was striped in various ways; or the parti-colouring would assume various forms, as a zig-zag on the thigh, or calf, or both; in fact, the leg was regarded as a field for the dress designer to exercise his ingenuity in the matter of contrast, upon the principle of what is known in ornament as counterchange.

ANGLO-SAXON RETAINER (G. W. RHEAD).

In Field's play of "A Woman is a Weathercock," 1612, one of the characters exclaims, "Indeed, there's reason there should be some difference in my legs, for one cost me twenty pounds more than the other."

At the beginning of the sixteenth century a new development appears, which began as an upper garment reaching only to the knees, also at this period called hose, upper stocks, and "trawses," which were puffed, slashed, and embroidered in various ways; this was the precursor of the *breeches*, or trunk-hose, which by the end of the century had developed to such enormous proportions.

Numerous examples of the "slashed" period will be found in the drawings by Holbein and Durer, and the engravings by Hans Burgkmair. The "slashings," which may be regarded as ornament *in relief*, presented as many variations as did the flat ornament of the earlier period on the plain surface of the leg. The garment was either slashed downwards, horizontally, or diagonally, and occasionally slashed to such an extent that it appeared merely as a system of ribbons. Variety of colour was arrived at either by the under-garment, stocking, or hose being of a different hue to the upper; or by a system of puffing, in which another or third colour was introduced. The puffing was also of a different material, either of silk or other light material, while the upper or slashing was of cloth or velvet.

It was an exceedingly rich, ornate, and fantastic period; the *jerkin*, or body garment, together with the sleeves, were also cut and slashed on the same principle as the lower garment, or *vice versâ*, the slashings on the body usually appearing diagonally on either side. In two female portraits, however, by Holbein at Basle, the slashings appear perpendicularly underneath the breast, the sleeve being slashed on the same principle.

The greatest richness of slashing always appears in the sleeve, a common form being to slash the sleeve in ribbons, which hang loose from the shoulder to the elbow. In the instances of several of the foot soldiers in Hans Burgkmair's "Triumphs of Maximilian," the outer sleeve is simply cut to ribbons, which stream loosely from the shoulder; and it seems, indeed, a little curious that at present, when all sorts of devices are employed for the purpose of producing variety, that some fashion of this sort has not been adopted for women. It represents, however, the most extreme development of the slash; it would be impossible to carry the principle farther.

We now arrive at the period of the enormous trunk-hose, *temp*. Elizabeth and James I., of which an example of their highest development appears in the illustration of "Knightly Pastimes—Hawking, 1575," and in which the middle of the body appears inflated like a balloon, the "bombasting" of the breeches being carried to its utmost limit. Their gipcieres are well in evidence in each instance. This article of costume was, no doubt, originally a game bag, but was afterwards generally used as a pocket or pouch—

> "An anlas and a gipser al of silke
> Heng at his gerdul white as morne mylke."

Chaucer.

The trunk-hose are, according to Stubbes ("Anatomy of Abuse"), of three kinds—the French, the Gallic, and the Venetian hosen. The French hose "are of two divers making; the common sort contain length, breadth, and sideness sufficient, and they are made very round; the other sort contain neither length, breadth, nor sideness proportionable, being not past a quarter of a yard on the side, whereof some be paned or striped, cut and drawn out with costly ornaments, with *canions* adjoined, reaching down beneath the knees.

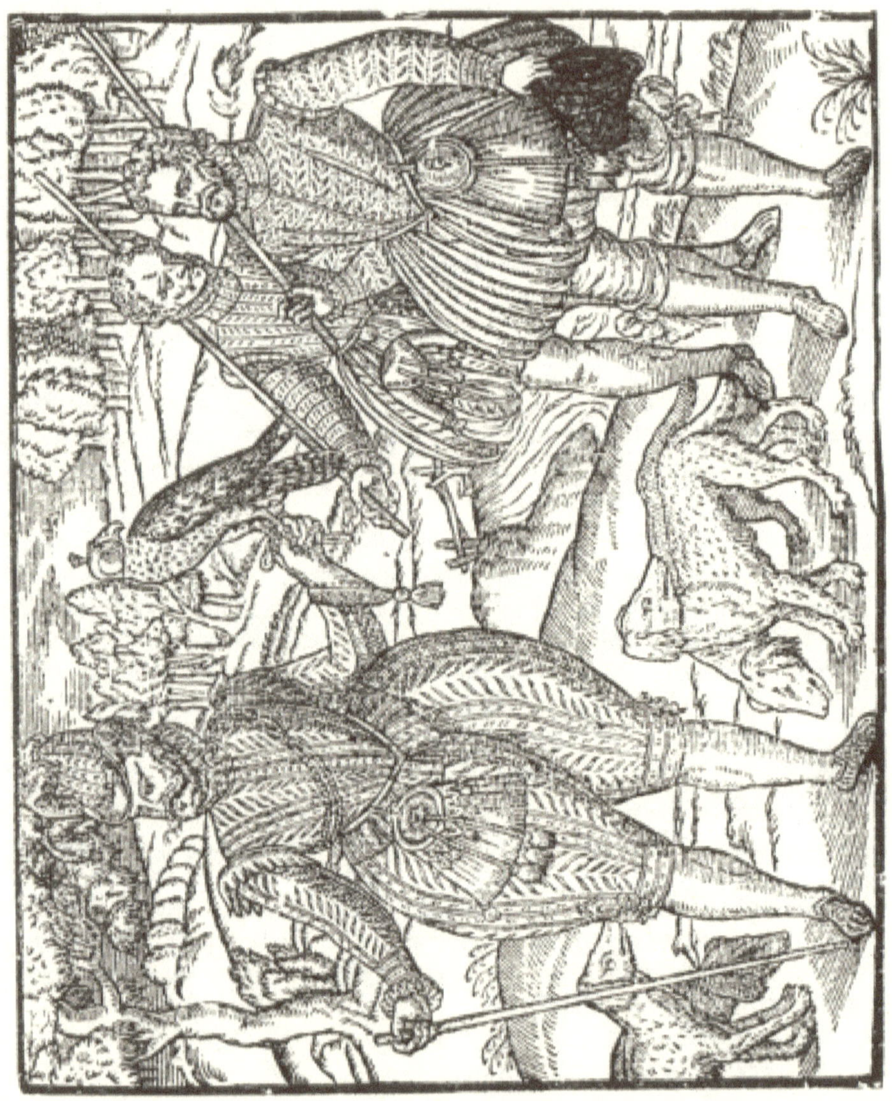

KNIGHTLY PASTIMES: HAWKING, 1575.

"The Gallic hosen are made very large and wide, reaching down to the knees only, with three or four gardes apiece laid down along the thigh of either hose. The Venetian hosen reach beneath the knee to the gartering-place of the leg, where they are tied finely with silken points, and laid on also with rows or gardes, as the other before. And yet notwithstanding, all this is not sufficient, except they be made of silk, velvet, satin, damask, and other precious stuffs besides; so that it is a small matter to bestow twenty nobles, ten pounds, twenty pounds, forty pounds, yea, an hundred pounds, upon one pair of breeches; and yet this is thought no abuse neither."

It has been stated by various writers that silk hose, *i.e.*, stockings of silk, were unknown in England prior to the middle of the sixteenth century. However this may be, silk stockings were, in the reign of Edward VI., considered as a gift worthy of a king's acceptance; it is recorded that Sir Thomas Gresham (whose portrait appears on p. 121) presented this monarch with a pair of long Spanish silk hose.

SIR THOMAS GRESHAM, 1519-1579. (NATIONAL PORTRAIT GALLERY).

Sir Antonio More, National Portrait Gallery.

Photo by Emery Walker.

In the inventory of the wardrobe of Henry VIII., taken after his decease, appears: "One pair of short hose, of black silk and gold woven together; one pair of hose, of purple silk and Venice gold, woven like unto a cawl, and lined with blue silver sarsenet, edged with a passemain of purple silk and of gold, wrought at Milan; one pair of hose of white silk and gold knit, bought of Christopher Millener; six pair of black silk hose knit."

PHILIP II. OF SPAIN, 1527-1598. (NATIONAL PORTRAIT GALLERY).

National Portrait Gallery.

Photo by Emery Walker.

We learn from Stow that Mistress Montague, the Queen's silk-woman, presented Elizabeth with "a pair of black knit silk stockings, which pleased her so well, that she would never wear any cloth hose afterwards."

The "bombasting" of the trunk-hose (the word is usually applied to the doublet, but may be applied equally well to the trunk-hose) was effected by means of a stuffing of rags, wool, tow, hair, and even bran. Holinshed relates a story of a man "who is said to have exhibited the whole of his bed and table furniture, taken from these extensive receptacles." The name trunk-hose would seem a peculiarly appropriate one! The story is probably apocryphal (although quite plausible) of the young man who, engaged in animated, and apparently rather excited conversation with several ladies, caught his trunk-hose in a nail, and let out the bran, the hose collapsing suddenly, to the consternation of their wearer and the corresponding amusement of the ladies.

Ben Jonson, "Every Man out of his Humour," thus recounts a misfortune which happened to Fastidio in a duel: "I had on a gold cable hatband, then new come up, of massie goldsmith's work, which I wore about a murrey French hat, the brims of which were thick embroidered with gold twist and spangles; I had an Italian cut-work band, ornamented with pearls, which cost three pounds at the Exchange.... He, making a reverse blow, falls upon my embossed girdle—I had thrown off the hangers a little before; strikes off a skirt of a thick satin doublet I had, lined with four taffataes; cuts off two panes of embroidered pearls; rends through the drawings out of tissue; enters the lining, and skips the flesh; and not having leisure to put off my silver spurs, one of the rowels catched hold of the ruffle of my boot, it being Spanish leather, and subject to tear; overthrows me, and rends me two pairs of stockings, that I had put on being a raw morning—a peach-colour and another."

In the same play, Fungoso, reckoning up the price of Fastidio's dress, says: "Let me see; the doublet—say fifty shillings the doublet—and between three and four pounds the hose,—then the boots, hat, and band;—some ten or eleven pounds will do it all."

By the year 1583 the trunks are rifled of their contents in order to provide stuffing for the doublet. It will be noticed in the cut of knightly pastimes that the girdle meets at a point in front. This shape was emphasised, the doublet protruded in front, and hung down for some distance, and the peas-cod bellied doublet was developed. We must again turn to our old "anatomist" Stubbes: "Certain I am there was never any kind of apparel invented that could more disproportion the body of a man than their doublets with great bellies do, hanging down beneath the groin, as I have said, and stuffed with four or five, or six pounde of bombast at the least. I say nothing of what their doublets be made; some of satin, taffata, silk, grograine, chamlet, gold, silver, and what not; slashed, jagged, cut, carved, pinched, and laced with all kinds of costly lace of divers and sundry colours, of all which, if I could stand upon particularly, rather time than matter would be wanting." The peas-cod bellied doublet is still perpetuated in the person of our esteemed contemporary, Mr. Punch.

An excellent example of the trunk-hose of the latter part of the reign of James I. appears in the engraved portrait of Henry, Prince of Wales. The hose consists of a series of richly embroidered straps discovering the silk or velvet trunk in the narrow intervals between.

ILLUSTRISSIMI GENEROSISSIMIQUE PRI. HENRICI MAGNÆ
BRITANNIÆ ET HYBERNIÆ PRINCIPIS, Vera Effigies.

HENRY, PRINCE OF WALES.

Engraved by Simon Passe, 1612.

With the reign of the "martyr King" Charles, both peas-cod bellied doublets
and trunk-hose disappear, and the costume of this period is strikingly picturesque. Charles was a man of cultivated taste, and handsome to boot; he undoubtedly influenced the costume of his time. The earliest engraved portraits, by Francis
Delaram and William Hole, exhibit him in long, loose breeches reaching to the
knees, with the doublet still pointed at the waist. The more familiar costume of
this monarch is, however, that which is seen in the various portraits by Vandyke.
The costume of the Cavaliers is well described in a little book on British costume
published in the "Library of Entertaining Knowledge" in 1834: "It consisted of a

doublet of silk, satin, or velvet, with large loose sleeves, slashed up the front; the collar, covered by a falling band of the richest point lace, with that peculiar edging now called Vandyke; a short cloak was worn carelessly on one shoulder. The long breeches, fringed or pointed, as we have already mentioned, met the tops of the wide boots, which were also ruffled with lace or lawn. A broad-leafed Flemish beaver hat, with a rich hatband and plume of feathers, was set on one side of the head, and a Spanish rapier, hung from a magnificent baldrick or sword-belt, worn sashwise over the right shoulder."

We now arrive at the period of the dandiacal Pepys, who describes with great unction the various changes and details of his costume. On September 13, 1660, the Duke of Gloucester died of the small-pox "by the great negligence of the doctors." He was buried on the 21st at Westminster, and on the 22nd our chronicler "purchased a pair of short black stockings to wear over a pair of silk ones for mourning." On April 23, 1661, the occasion of the King's going from the Tower to Whitehall, he rose with the lark, made himself as fine as he could, and put on his velvet coat, the first day that he put it on, "though made half a year ago."

"*September 29th, 1661.*—This day I put on my half cloth black stockings, and my new coate of the fashion, which pleases me well, and with my beaver I was (after office was done) ready to go to my Lord Mayor's feast, as we were all invited."

The long laced coats, familiar during the latter part of the reign of the "Merry Monarch" and the succeeding reign, had already come into vogue. On May 11, 1662, Pepys repaired in the afternoon to Whitehall, and "walked in the parke," where he saw the King, "now out of mourning in a suit laced with gold and silver, which it was said was out of fashion."

The costume of the masses during the Commonwealth and Restoration, was the well-known knee breeches and stockings, with doublet or jerkin.

In a poem called "Wit Restored," *c.* 1658, is described the holiday dress of a countryman when courting:—

> "And first chill put on my Zunday parell
> That's lac't about the Quarters;
> With a pair of buckram slopps,
> And a vlanting pair of garters.
> With a sword tide vast to my side,
> And my grandfather's dugen and dagger,
> And a peacock's veather in my capp,
> Then, oh, how I shall swagger!"

About the year 1658 petticoat breeches crossed the silver streak from Versailles, and became the vogue at the Court of Charles II. Randal Holme, writing in 1659, describes the dress as follows:—"A short-waisted doublet and petticoat breeches, the lining being lower than the breeches and tied above the knees; the breeches are ornamented with ribands up to the pocket, and half their breadth upon the thigh; the waistband is set about with ribands, and the shirt hanging out over them." The petticoat breeches were not ridiculous in themselves—the modern Scotch kilt, which is an extremely picturesque and even reasonable costume, is made upon precisely the same principle; it was the absurd lace ruffles, which hung drooping below the knee, which were worn with the petticoats during the earlier period, and in which Charles II. is figured in Heath's Chronicle, 1662, which made the costume a banality. The figure of the exquisite of 1670 from Jacquemin wears the petticoat breeches, but without the ruffles or frills at the knees. It must be confessed, however, that the gentleman possesses a sufficiency of frill!

AN EXQUISITE (FROM JACQUEMIN).

From Jacquemin.

Petticoat breeches had disappeared by the end of the reign of Charles II., and we have now to deal with another distinct change in the national costume. In an inventory of apparel of Charles II. in 1679 appears a suit of clothes of one material, and consisting of *coat*, waistcoat, and breeches. William III. is figured in 1694 in a long laced coat with enormous sleeve cuffs, the waistcoat almost as long as the coat, with large flaps and pockets also richly laced, the nether garments being knee breeches and stockings with buckled shoes, the hat cocked according to the fancy of the wearer. This coat, indeed, has, with variations, existed up to the present time. The gold lacings, the rows of buttons down the front, the huge cuffs, indeed, have vanished; but the modern coat is, fundamentally, the same as its earliest prototype. The two buttons at the back, which now serve no purpose other than an ornamental one, once buttoned up the flaps, and constitute the last remains of the coat's former glories.

PHILIPPE DE VENDÔME, GRAND PRIEUR DE FRANCE.

From an old print in the British Museum.

Towards the middle of the eighteenth century the coat fits tightly to the body, the skirts being long and ample, and made to stand out stiffly by being lined with buckram; the large Kevenhuller hat has given place to one of much more moderate proportions.

The fop of the day is thus ridiculed by Diana in the play of "Lionel and Clarissa," by Isaac Bickerstaff, 1768: —

"Ladies, pray admire a figure,
Fait selon le dernier gout.
First, his hat, in size no bigger
Than a Chinese woman's shoe;
Six yards of ribbon bind
His hair en baton behind;
While his foretop's so high,
That in the crown he may vie
With the tufted cockatoo.
Then his waist so long and taper
'Tis an absolute thread-paper:
Maids, resist him, you that can.
Odd's life, if this is all th' affair,
I'll clap a hat on, club my hair,
And call myself a man."

The short hair and large bishop's sleeves of the clergy are satirised in the same play: —

"Lauk! Madam, do you think, when Mr. Lionel's a clergyman, he'll be obliged to cut off his hair? I'm sure it will be a thousand pities, for it is the sweetest colour! and your great pudding-sleeves, Lord! they'll quite spoil his shape, and the fall of his shoulders. Well, Madam, if I was a lady of large fortune, I'll be hanged if Mr. Lionel should be a parson, if I could help it."

V
THE KIRTLE OR PETTICOAT

"*Falstaff.* What trade art thou, Feeble?

"*Feeble.* A woman's tailor, sir.

"*Shallow.* Shall I prick him, sir?

"*Falstaff.* You may; but if he had been a man's tailor he would have pricked you—Wilt thou make as many holes in an enemy's battle, as thou hast done in a woman's petticoat?

"*Feeble.* I will do my good will, sir; you can have no more.

"*Falstaff.* Well said, good woman's tailor! well said, courageous Feeble! Thou wilt be as valiant as the wrathful dove, or most magnanimous mouse—Prick the woman's tailor well, Master Shallow; deep, Master Shallow."

V

THE KIRTLE OR PETTICOAT

The kirtle or petticoat is in reality a development of the tunic. It is the tunic which has become a closely fitting bodice, with long draperies, more or less formal, attached. The names of the different portions of dress have at different periods varied almost indefinitely. The first item of the habit of the Order of the Garter is successively described as tunic, coat, surcoat, and *kirtle*.

The kirtle, therefore, takes up the story of costume from the time when the loose tunic gave place to a more formal attire—broadly speaking, from the Norman Conquest.

During the eleventh century, however, woman's dress was still the loose tunic, the principal change being in the remarkable development of the sleeves, which, although close fitting along the whole length of the arm, either had an extraordinary attachment at the wrist in the form of a bag or pouch, or were abnormally extended and widened at the wrist and tied in knots to avoid treading on them. This fashion is satirised in the figure of the devil from the Cotton MSS., given in the introductory chat of this work.

In the "Romaunt of the Rose," written at the close of the thirteenth century, John de Meun relates the story of Pygmalion, representing him as adorning the statue he had created with a succession of the garments of the fashion of the period of the poem, with the purpose of discovering which became her best:—"He clothed her in many guises; in robes, made with great skill, of the finest silk and woollen cloths; green, azure, and brunette, ornamented with the richest skins of ermines, minivers, and greys: these being taken off, other robes were tried upon her, of silk, cendal, mallequins, mallebruns, satins, diaper, and camelot, and all of divers colours. Thus decorated, she resembled a little angel; her countenance was so modest. Then, again, he put a wimple upon her head, and over that a coverchief, which concealed the wimple, but hid not her face. All these garments were then laid aside for gowns, yellow, red, green, and blue; and her hair was handsomely disposed in small braids, with threads of silk and gold adorned with little pearls, upon which was placed, with great precision, a crestine; and over the crestine, a crown or circle of gold, enriched with precious stones of various sizes. Her little ears were decorated with two beautiful pendants of gold, and her necklace was confined to her neck by two clasps of gold. Her girdle was exceedingly rich, and to it was attached an aulmoniere, or small purse, of great value."

In the reign of Edward III. the close-fitting bodice appears, with the girdle over the hips, the sleeves either tight or provided with an upper sleeve with long tippets or streamers from the elbow. Later a kind of "spencer"[13] jacket, or waistcoat, was worn, faced and bordered with miniver or other fur. These "spencer"-like jackets lasted for a considerable period. An example appears in the effigy of Joan of Navarre, Queen of Henry IV. A similar jacket again appears in the reign of Henry VI.

**THE CLOSE FITTING JACKET TEMP. EDWARD III.
(FROM VIOLLET LE DUC).**

Temp. Edward III.

The Italian *cassone*, or marriage chests, of the fourteenth and fifteenth centuries, furnish us with many examples of graceful dresses of a character peculiar to that period and nation, but which fashion obtained to some extent elsewhere; a good deal of the grace of these things is due, however, to the fine convention adopted in the work of this period. A feature of this dress is the long wide sleeves streaming from the shoulders, part sleeve and part cloak. The illustration which forms the heading of Chat IV. will serve to give some idea of this dress.

At the commencement of the Tudor period the costume of the ladies is still that of the period of high head-dresses of the middle of the century. The waist is still high and narrow, the gown long, ample and flowing, often edged with fur,

---

[13] The term "spencer" is a modern one, and is said to originate from an accident to Lord Spencer, in which he lost his coat-tails during a hunt, *temp.* George III.

and with fur collar and cuffs. By the end of the reign of Henry VIII., however, costume had undergone a marked change. The waist suddenly drops, the stomacher appears, together with the bell-shaped open gown, with richly embroidered petticoat, which lasted for a considerable time—to the time of Charles I., in fact. Both cut gown and inner petticoat were ornamented, either by woven patterns or embroidery, the richest ornaments being reserved for the petticoat; the turnovers or "collars" of the skirts being plain, in contrast to the rich ornaments of the upper surface.

An interesting portrait of Queen Mary (Red Mary) by Lucas de Heere, in the possession of Sir William Quilter, was recently shown at the exhibition at the Guildhall of the works of Flemish painters. She wears a black dress with stiffened collar behind, ornamented with gold embroidery, open at the neck, disclosing a pink bodice also richly embroidered, the sleeves furred at the elbows.

The era of petticoat inflation began about this time; it was such a remarkable development that the consideration of it is reserved for a separate chat.

In Holinshed's Chronicle, 1577, appears an amusing cut of "Makbeth and Banquho" met by "the iij weird Sisters or Feiries." "Makbeth" is figured as wearing an astonishing Life Guard helmet and plume. "The iij weird Feiries" are fascinating creatures, gaily dressed in ornamented kirtles, with panniers, puffed sleeves and shoulders, and, in one instance, with a remarkable peaked turban with streamer on her head.

The dress of the Tudor period was magnificent beyond description. In a wardrobe account of Henry VIII., seven yards of purple cloth-of-gold damask is apportioned for a kirtle for Catherine of Arragon. As in the case of the men, the sleeves were invariably the richest portion of women's dress. "Amongst the inventories of this reign we find: three pair of purple satin sleeves for women; one pair of linen sleeves, paned with gold over the arm, quilted with black silk, and wrought with flowers between the panes and at the hands; one pair of sleeves of purple gold tissue damask wire, each sleeve tied with aglets of gold; one pair of crimson satin sleeves, four buttons of gold being set on each sleeve, and in every button nine pearls."

This extravagance was more than continued during the reign of Elizabeth. It is thus satirised by Beaumont and Fletcher in "Four Plays in One."

> "I went then to Vanity, whom I found
> Attended by an endless troop of taylors,
> Mercers, embroiderers, feather-makers, fumers;
> All occupations opening like a mart,
> That serve to rig the body out with bravery;
> And through the room new fashions flew like flies,
> In thousand gaudy shapes; Pride waiting on her,
> And busily surveying all the breaches
> Time and decaying nature had wrought in her,
> Which still with art she piec'd again, and strengthened.
> I told your wants; she shew'd me gowns and headtires,

Embroider'd waste coats, smocks seamed through with cut-work,
Scarfs, mantles, petticoats, muffs, powders, paintings,
Dogs, monkies, parrots; all of which seem'd to show me
The way her money went."

A LADY OF BASLE (HOLBEIN).

Holbein.

The beauties of the Court of the Merry Monarch are made familiar to us by the pencil of Sir Peter Lely.[14] The age was distinguished in the case of the women not so much for the magnificence of its costume as for the scantiness of it. It was to a certain extent a return to the simplicity of Nature!

"If," says Addison, writing in the *Spectator*, "we survey the pictures of our great-grandmothers in Queen Elizabeth's time, we see them clothed down to the very wrists, and up to the very chin. The hands and face were the only samples they gave of their beautiful persons. The following age of females made larger discoveries of their complexion. They first of all tucked up their garments to the elbow, and, notwithstanding the tenderness of the sex, were content for the information of mankind to expose their arms to the coldness of the air, and injuries of the weather."

They affected a mean between dress and nakedness, which occasioned the publication of a book entitled "A Just and Seasonable Reprehension of Naked Breasts and Shoulders," with a preface by Richard Baxter, *temp.* Charles II.

Herrick's lines may be said to foreshadow the period:—

> "A sweet disorder in the dress
> Kindles in clothes a wantonness;
> A lawn about the shoulders thrown
> Into a fine distraction;
> An erring lace, which here and there
> Enthrals the crimson stomacher;
> A cuff neglected, and thereby
> Ribbons to flow confusedly;
> A winning wave, deserving note
> In the tempestuous petticoat.
> A careless shoe-string, in whose tie
> I see a wild civility;—
> Do more bewitch me, than when art
> Is too precise in every part."

The remarks of our diarist Pepys on the subject of dress are always entertaining, although he displays perhaps less interest in his wife's dresses than in his own.

"*April 15th, 1662.*—With my wife, by coach, to the new Exchange, to buy her some things; where we saw some new-fashion petticoats of sarcanett with a black broad lace printed round the bottom and before, very handsome, and my wife had a mind to one of them."

His wife's dressmaker's bill is apparently a much less serious item than his own dress expenses, which is perhaps the reverse of the present order of things.

---

[14] "This day I did first see the Duke of York's room of pictures of some Maids of Honour, done by Lilly; good, but not like."—*Pepys's Diary.*

THE CHILDREN OF CHARLES I.

After Vandyck. Engraved by Sir Robert Strange.

"*October 30th, 1663.* — To my great sorrow find myself £43 worse than I was the last month.... But it hath chiefly arisen from my layings-out in clothes for myself and wife; viz., for her about £12, and for myself £55—or thereabouts,(!) having made myself a velvet cloak, two new cloth skirts, a new shag gown, trimmed with gold buttons and twist, with a new hat, and silk tops for my legs, and many other things, being resolved, henceforward, to go like myself"(!!).

"*March 2nd, 1669.* — My wife this day put on her first French gown, called a Sac, which becomes her very well."

May Day of the same year: "My wife extraordinary fine with her flowered tabby gown that she made two years ago, now laced exceeding pretty; and indeed was fine all over. And mighty earnest to go, though the day was very lowering; and she would have me put on my fine suit—which I did"(!).

A certain affectation by the ladies of male costume made its appearance towards the close of the century. Laced and buttoned coats and waistcoats were worn, together with a smartly cocked hat surmounted with a feather. It also appeared earlier, during the reign of Elizabeth, and was satirised by Stubbes, and later, in the *Spectator*, by Addison. We picture Die Vernon in a habit of this kind, which was chiefly worn for riding, but also for walking. Fielding describes the appearance of Sophia Western at the inn at Upton in a similar habit.

MISS LEWIS.

Engraved by James Macardell.

The rigidity of the bodice at the commencement of the Hanoverian period was an echo of an earlier time, when Good Queen Bess strutted it in wheeled farthingale. It was strongly fortified with whalebone strips, and formed a V in front.

One of the chief characteristics of the dresses of this period was the naturalistic floral patternings, which were seen everywhere, and even invaded the dress of the men, whose waistcoats were gay with embroidered flowers. This floral patterning was the outward and visible sign of the general interest which was then taken in natural form. Linnæus, at Upsala, was propounding his botanical system; gardening was generally popular. Mrs. Delany thus describes a dress which she saw at Court in February, 1741, and which is sufficiently indicative of the generally prevailing taste: "The Duchess of Queensberry's clothes pleased me best; they were white satin embroidered—the bottom of the petticoat brown hills covered with all sorts of weeds, and every breadth had an old stump of a tree that ran up almost to the top of the petticoat, broken and ragged and worked with brown chenille, round which twined nastersians, ivy, honeysuckles, periwinkles, convolvuluses, and all sorts of twining flowers, which spread and covered the petticoat; vines with the leaves variegated as you have seen them by the sun, all rather smaller than nature, which makes them look very light; the robings and facings were little green banks with all sorts of weeds; and the sleeves and the rest of the gown loose, twining branches of the same sort as those on the petticoat. Many of the leaves were finished with gold, and part of the stumps of the trees looked like the gilding of the sun."

THE GAMUT OF LOVE (WATTEAU).

From an engraving after Watteau.

The quilted petticoat with figured panniers which is associated with the name of Dolly Varden is a charming dress of the rustic or idyllic sort. Like the rigid bodice, it was a development of the dress of an earlier period; it was, in fact, the stiff outer kirtle of the Elizabethan and Stuart periods looped up in folds.

The fashionable luxuries of the latter half of the eighteenth century are thus commented upon in the *London Magazine* of February, 1773:—

"The modes of dress, as well as those of house-keeping, are articles of incredible expense. Here the ladies are beyond description extravagant.

"They have spring and summer, autumn and winter silks; brocades, gold and silver stuffs; some of which are bought at the enormous price of thirty guineas a yard. The birthday suit is never worn a second time. Their heads are adorned with Dresden and Mechlin lace, enriched with jewels of immense value: large estates hang upon their ears. How brilliant are their diamond necklaces and stomachers, their watches, and other trinkets!—their very buckles are set with pearls and precious stones."

A character in "Bon Ton; or, High Life Above Stairs," by David Garrick, 1775, exclaims:—

"This fellow would turn rake and maccaroni if he was to stay here a week longer—bless me, what dangers are in this town at every step! O, that I were once settled safe again at Trotley-place!—nothing to save my country would bring me back again: my niece, Lucretia, is so be-fashioned and be-devilled, that nothing, I fear, can save her; however, to ease my conscience, I must try; but what can be expected from the young women of these times, but sallow looks, wild schemes, saucy words, and loose morals!—they lie a-bed all day, sit up all night; if they are silent they are gaming; and if they talk, 'tis either scandal or infidelity; and that they may look what they are, their heads are all feather, and round their necks are twisted rattlesnake tippets—O tempora, O mores!"

In the *Lady's Magazine* for April, 1782, the following announcement of fashionable dress at Paris is given:—

"The Queen of France has appeared at Versailles in a morning dress that has totally eclipsed the levée robe, and is said to be the universal rage. The robe is made of plain sattin, chiefly white, worn without a hoop, round, and a long train. It is drawn up in the front, on one side, and fastened with tassels of silver, gold, or silk, according to the taste of the wearer; and this discloses a puckered petticoat of gauze or sarsenet, of a different colour. The sleeves are wide and short, drawn up near the shoulder with small tassels, or knots of diamonds; under sleeves of the finest cambrick, full plaited, and trimmed at the elbow with Brussels or point, give infinite charms to the whole. The fastening of the waist is not straight down the stays, but gently swerved, and trimmed with narrow fur, as is the bottom of the robe. A round pasteboard hat, covered with the same sattin, and without any other ornaments than a diamond buckle, or an embroidered one, finishes the dress, which, it is said, will be worn through the summer, made of lighter materials."

The French Revolution was productive of many things—not the least of which was the change it brought in the matter of dress. The revival of classicism in costume during the Empire, which was to a great extent due to the influence of the painter David, was an echo of the earlier classic revival in architecture, mainly represented in this country by the work of the brothers Adam, who designed, as well as architecture, carriages, furniture, plate, and even a sedan chair for Queen Charlotte. With the advent of the Revolution the fashion suddenly changes. The oft-quoted couplet—

"Shepherds, I have lost my waist;
Have ye seen my body?"

a parody on a popular song, "The Banks of Banna"—expresses the disappearance of that portion of the body, which had previously been absurdly long. The ample flowered skirts of the middle of the century gave place to light gauze clinging coverings which exhibited as much of Nature's form as was—desirable. The *merveilleuses* appeared in gossamer gowns, slit from the hips and buttoned at the knees after the fashion of the Macedonian girls alluded to in a previous chat, the legs encased in fleshings. "Behold her, that beautiful citoyenne, in costume of the ancient Greeks, such Greek as painter David could teach; her sweeping tresses snooded by glittering antique fillet; bright-dyed tunic of the Greek woman; her little feet naked as in antique statues, with mere sandals and winding strings of riband—defying the frost."[15]

MADAME DE MOUCHY, IN BALL DRESS.

Engraved by Pierre-Louis Surugue.

---

[15] Carlyle.

"English Costume from Pocket-books," 1799, tells of a Russian officer, who, having been accustomed at home to estimate the rank of a lady by the *warmth* of her clothing, offered a woman of fashion a penny, in Bond Street, under the impression that from her nakedness she must be a pauper!

WALKING DRESS, 1810.

The Empire gown is figured in the illustration of a walking dress, 1810. It lasted practically until the advent of the crinoline in the forties, when it finally disappeared. There has been recent talk of its revival, but dancing men are found to be opposed to it, if for no other reason than the difficulty of knowing where to place their arms; and dancing men are apparently a necessity.

The really fashionable people are those who are not in the fashion. This may at first sight seem a paradox, but a moment's consideration will be sufficiently convincing. The Empress of Germany gives an order to her dressmaker for four dresses, on the strict understanding that no others are to be made like them (*vide* daily paper). *This* is the genuine woman of fashion. The people who are "in the fashion" are the sheep. "Bell-wether takes the leap and they all jump over." In other words, there can be no really beautiful dress unless the spirit of individualism is fostered. Dress should "express" the wearer and provide an index as to character. Indeed, it does, as the spectacle of a woman or a man following blindly the dictates of fashion is sufficient evidence that he or she possesses no character at all.

There is also a manner of dressing and of wearing, a certain elegance that distinguishes people of taste from the vulgar, which gives each portion of the dress its due importance, and imparts a harmony to the whole, as in the composition of a picture, which weaves every detail into one design and impresses the beholder as a masterpiece.

PROMENADE COSTUME, 1833.

Moreover, there is a charm and piquancy of manner quite apart from the dress itself, or even the personal beauty of the wearer, which distinguishes the fascinating woman. A character in "The Belle's Stratagem" exclaims—with what degree of truth the reader himself must determine:

"Pho! thou hast no taste! English beauty! 'tis insipidity: it wants the zest, it wants poignancy, Frank! Why, I have known a Frenchwoman, indebted to Nature for no one thing but a pair of decent eyes, reckon in her suit as many counts, marquisses, and petits maîtres, as would satisfy three dozen of our first-rate toasts. I have known an Italian marquizina make ten conquests in stepping from her carriage, and carry her slaves from one city to another, whose real intrinsic beauty would have yielded to half the little grisettes that pace your Mall on a Sunday."

PARIS EVENING DRESS, 1833.

VI
THE RISE AND FALL
OF THE CRINOLINE

"For I will goe frocked and in a French hood,
I will have my fine cassockes and my round verdingale."
Booke of Robin Conscience.

THE CRINOLINE (HEADING: FIGURE FROM JACQUEMIN).

From Jacquemin.

VI

THE RISE AND FALL OF THE CRINOLINE

Fielding, in his description of the beauty and many graces of Sophia Western, feeling his subject to be more than ordinarily sublime, introduces his hero-
ine "with the utmost solemnity, with an elevation of style, and all the other circumstances proper to raise the veneration of the reader": "Hushed be every ruder
breath. May the heathen ruler of the winds confine in iron chains the boisterous
limbs of noisy Boreas, and the sharp-pointed nose of bitter-biting Eurus. Do thou,
sweet Zephyrus, rising from thy fragrant bed, mount the western sky and lead
on those delicious gales, the charms of which call forth the lovely Flora from her
chamber, perfumed with pearly dews, when on the first of June, her birthday, the
blooming maid, in loose attire, gently trips it over the verdant mead, where every
flower rises to do her homage, until the whole field becomes enamelled, and colours contend with sweets which shall ravish her most.

"So charming may she now appear; and you, the feathered choristers of
nature, whose sweetest notes not even Handel can excel, tune your melodious
throats to celebrate her appearance. *From love proceeds your music, and to love it returns.* Awake, therefore," &c.

If one were fortunate enough to possess the power of description and imagination of a Fielding, methinks the crinoline would provide a sufficiently inspiring
theme.

QUEEN CHARLOTTE (AFTER GAINSBOROUGH).

After Gainsborough.

It has been said that Milton was a man from his birth. The crinoline, like Milton, is an exception to every law of development. It had, like Milton, neither infancy nor adolescence, but sprang full armed, like "Athene from the brain of

Zeus," or perhaps, like Topsy in "Uncle Tom's Cabin," it never was born, but just "growed"—and it grew—like a mushroom (which indeed in form it somewhat resembles), in a night. Or, to adopt yet another comparison, like the sun, which bursts in the morning suddenly in its full refulgence, is obscured for a time by clouds, to blaze again in unabated splendour, and in its turn is again obscured, but only to reappear in glorious sunset.

The crinoletta, which followed, may be described as the twilight or sweet afterglow—beautiful, tender as the blush on a maiden's cheek, and almost as evanescent, but with none of the glory of the preceding day.

In the charming passage from Fielding above quoted, Love, it will be seen, figures as the presiding spirit. This is peculiarly appropriate to the present subject, for, be it known, *Dan Cupid begat the crinoline*. It is said to have been originally invented for the purpose of concealing the illicit amours of a Princess of Spain; but singularly enough, and in a sort of contradictory spirit, is first identified with the august person of the "Maiden Queen."

The earlier portraits of Elizabeth exhibit her in a dress similar to that of her sister and predecessor, and in an interesting portrait of Catherine Parr at Glendon Hall, Northamptonshire, this Queen appears in a richly embroidered petticoat widened at the base. A similar petticoat or kirtle, widened a little at the hips, is shown in the portrait of Mary, Queen of Scots, with Darnley (p. 169). The hooped petticoat or *vardingale*, however, appears only in the later portraits of Elizabeth. In the famous print by William Rogers, of which a reproduction is given, she is figured in the great ruff with which she is most identified, the interminable stomacher, and the enormous wheel farthingale, with, as Walpole observes, "a bushel of pearls bestrewed over the entire figure"; she also wears a long light mantle edged with lace, a portentous collar, also edged with lace, expanding like wings on either side of the head. She carries the ball and sceptre in her hands.

The legend at the foot of the plate runs as follows:—

> "The admired Empresse through the worlde applauded
> For supreme virtues rarest imitation,
> Whose Scepters rule fame's loud-voyc'd trumpet lawdeth
> Into the eares of every forraigne nation.
> Cannopey'd under powerfull angells winges
> To her Immortall praise sweete Science singes."

The great wheel farthingale was worn by the nobility during the latter half of the reign of Elizabeth, and during the whole of the succeeding reign. The engraving by Renold Elstracke of James I. and his Queen, Anne of Denmark, shows the latter in a farthingale, which in size and general structure is identical with that worn by Elizabeth. It is, however, box pleated round the top of the drum, the farthingale being divided in front and discovering the kirtle underneath.

QUEEN ELIZABETH.

From an engraving by William Rogers.

The following story is told by Bulwer in his "Pedigree of the English Gallant": "When Sir Peter Wych was sent ambassador to the Grand Seignor from James I., his lady accompanied him to Constantinople, and the Sultaness having heard much of her, desired to see her; whereupon Lady Wych, attended by her waiting women, all of them dressed in their great vardingales, which was the Court-dress of the English ladies at that time, waited upon her highness. The Sultaness received her visitor with great respect, but, struck with the extraordinary extension of the hips of the whole party, seriously inquired if that shape was peculiar to the natural formation of English women, and Lady Wych was obliged to explain the whole mystery of the dress, in order to convince her that she and her companions were not really so deformed as they appeared to be."

JAMES I. AND HIS QUEEN, ANNE OF DENMARK.

From an engraving by R. Elstracke.

In the reign of Charles I. the farthingale, although still worn by the lower gentry and citizens' wives, is discarded by the upper classes, and disappears entirely; and it is not until the latter part of the reign of Queen Anne that it rises again, like the Phœnix from its own ashes, but in another form, however, that of the enormous hoop, which grew to such portentous proportions during the reigns of George I. and II., the outstanding steel or whalebone foundation being mainly at the bottom of the skirt instead of at the hips. Sir Roger de Coverley thus expresses the difference between the earlier hooped petticoats and those of the era of the *Spectator*: "You see, sir, my great-great-grandmother has on the new-fashioned petticoat, except that the modern is gathered at the waist; my grandmother appears as if she stood in a large drum, whereas the ladies now walk as if they were in a go-cart."

FESTAL DRESS, OTAHEITE.

It is surprising to find in dress, as in ornamental design, the same ideas, the same ornamental *motifs*, occurring to the people of countries widely separate. There is a curious dress appropriated to the young women of Otaheite who are appointed to make presents from persons of rank to each other; one of these was deputed to present cloths to Captain Cook on his last voyage. A representation of the dress is given in the engraving, which is from Cook's Geography, 1801. The proportions of the drum exceed even that of Queen Elizabeth; in general shape, however, it is similar. It is decorated round the uppermost edge with ornamental festoons of feathers, &c., and constitutes the complete dress of the lady, with the exception of a sort of chemise which appears underneath the breasts, and, presumably, covers the loins and a portion of the lower limbs.

PORTRAITS OF MARY, QUEEN OF SCOTS, AND DARNLEY.

From an engraving by R. Elstracke.

The hoop petticoat now approaches its highest meridian; its re-appearance was duly announced by Addison, who, in No. 129 of the *Spectator*, relates an adventure which happened in a little country church in Cornwall: "As we were in the midst of service, a lady, who is the chief woman of the place, and had passed the winter at London with her husband, entered the congregation in a little head-dress and a hooped petticoat. The people, who were wonderfully startled at such a sight, all of them rose up. Some stared at the prodigious bottom, and some at the little top, of this strange dress. In the meantime the lady of the manor *filled the area of the church* and walked up to the pew with an unspeakable satisfaction, amid the whispers, conjectures, and astonishments of the whole congregation."

Between 1740 and 1745 the hoops spread out at the sides extensively in oblong fashion, resembling a donkey carrying its panniers. Indeed, the simile of the donkey was a favourite one with the caricaturists. In 1860 *Punch* adopts the idea, and issues a warning to ladies who would ride in crinolines on donkeys, and gives a cut of a lady in an enormous crinoline riding on a donkey, with nothing but the donkey's hind legs seen below.

A poetic description of ladies' dresses in 1773 directs:

"Make your petticoats short, that a hoop eight yards wide
May decently show how your garters are tied."

Indeed, the hoop of this period had attained to such enormous proportions that, as Fairholt observes, the figure of a lady was considerable; for they were now not only the better, but the larger, half of creation, and half a dozen men might be accommodated in the space occupied by a single lady.[16]

"DON'T BE AFRAID, MY DEAR."

Engraved by Isidore-Stanilas Helman.

[16] Fairholt, "Costume in England."

In a print entitled "The Review," of the latter part of the reign of George II., the inconveniences of the hoop petticoat are exhibited in a variety of ways, and various methods for their remedy are suggested. One of the most ingenious is that of a coach with a moveable roof and a frame with pulleys to drop the ladies in from the top, in order to avoid the disarranging of their hoops which would necessarily attend their entrance by the door.

Hoop petticoats disappeared early in the reign of George III., and the genius of extravagance then turned its attention to the head-dress.

In the expiring years of the fifties of the last century the crinoline *proper* appeared. There had been hints of it earlier, not to say threats, in the bell-shaped skirts which obtained in about 1835, of which the charming creature in the London promenade dress (p. 55) provides an example.

The chief satirist of the crinoline is *Punch*, although, amongst others, an amusing skit on the difficulties and dangers of the crinoline appeared about 1870, with a number of coloured illustrations by "Quiz," now very rare.

Punch appears to have been particularly impressed by the "roomy" character of the crinoline, as, in an amusing if somewhat laboured skit in the early days of 1860, he unbosoms himself as follows:

"Among the million objections to the use of the wide petticoats not the least well-founded is the fact that they are used for purposes of shoplifting. This has many times been proved at the bar of the police courts, and we wonder that more notice has not been attracted to it. For ourselves, the fact is so impressed upon our mind, that when we ever come in contact with a Crinoline which seems more than usually wide, we immediately put down the wearer as a pick-pocket, and prepare ourselves at once to see her taken up. Viewing Crinoline, indeed, as an incentive to bad conduct, we forbid our wives and daughters to wear it when out shopping, for fear that it may tempt them to commit some act of theft. A wide petticoat is so convenient a hiding-place for stowing away almost any amount of stolen goods, that we cannot be surprised at finding it so used, and for the mere sake of keeping them from roguery, the fewer women have it at their fingers' ends the better. Some ladies have a monomania for thievery, and when they go on a day's shopping can hardly keep their hands off what does not belong to them. Having a commodious receptacle in reach, wherein they may deposit whatever they may sack, they are naturally tempted to indulge in their propensity, by the chances being lessened that they will be found out.

"As an instance of how largely the large petticoats are used in acts of petty larceny, we may mention a small fact which has come within our knowledge, and which it may be to the interest of shopkeepers to know. Concealed beneath the skirts of a fashionably dressed female were, the other day, discovered by a vigilant detective the following choice proofs of her propensity to plunder: viz., twenty-three shawls, eleven dozen handkerchiefs, sixteen pairs of boots (fifteen of them made up with the military heel), a case of eau-de-Cologne, a ditto of black hair-dye, thirty pairs of stays, twenty-six chemises, five dozen cambric handkerchiefs, and eleven ditto silk, nineteen muslin collars, and four-and-forty crochet ones, a dressing case, five hair brushes (three of them made with tortoiseshell and two with ivory gilt backs), a pair of curling irons, eight bonnets without trimmings and nine-and-twenty with them, a hundred rolls of ribbon, half a hundredweight of worsted, ten dozen white kid gloves and twenty dozen coloured ones, forty balls of cotton, nine-and-ninety skeins of silk, a gridiron, two coal-scuttles, three packets of ham sandwiches, twenty-five mince pies, half a leg of mutton, six boxes of French plums, ten ditto of bonbons, nine pâtés de foie gras, a dozen cakes of chocolate and nine of portable hare soup, a warming pan, five bracelets, a brace of large brass birdcages, sixteen bowls of goldfish, half a score of lapdogs, fourteen dozen lever watches, and an eight-day kitchen clock.

KING AND MRS. BADDELEY.

"After this discovery, who will venture to deny that Crinoline with shoplifters is comparable to charity, inasmuch as it may cover a multitude of sins?"

A curious advertisement in the *Illustrated London News* of October 10, 1863, announces that—"Ondina, or waved Jupons, do away with the unsightly results of the ordinary hoops, and so perfect are the wave-like bands that a lady may ascend a steep stair, lean against a table, throw herself into an armchair, pass to a stall in the opera, or occupy a fourth seat in a carriage without inconvenience to herself or to others, or provoking rude remarks of the observers, thus modifying in an important degree all those peculiarities tending to destroy the modesty of English women, and lastly, it allows the dress to fall into graceful folds. Price 21s. Illustrations free." With all these advantages, who would not wear a crinoline?

In the new year of 1860 *Punch* gives a cut ("Some good account at last") of a skater in pot-hat and pegtops, encircled by the framework of an enormous crinoline, cutting graceful figures upon the ice and exclaiming, "Entirely my own idea, Harry—ease, elegance, and safety combined—I call it the skater's friend." "Some good account at last"? Unkind Mr. Punch! Must we, then, measure the value of everything in this world by its bare utility? The crinoline will endure as a sweet solace to senses tired by the ennui of this dull earth. The memory of it will outlive the ages.

In the early seventies we find our old friend *Punch* again upon the warpath, and the Venus of Milo dons the crinoletta! This, however, is only a repetition of his satire on the crinoline in his "Essence of Parliament," May, 1860:—

"Lord Aberdeen's son, Lord Haddock, or some such name, made a supremely ridiculous speech upon the impropriety of allowing money to any school of Art in which the undraped she-model was studied from. His father, who was called Athenian Aberdeen, and has so earnest a love for Greek Art that he actually favoured Russia because she has a Greek Church, ought to have cured his Haddock of such nonsense. Poor old Mr. Spooner, naturally, took the same really indelicate view of the case. Sir George Lewis expressed his lofty contempt for the Haddock, and Lord Palmerston kippered him in a speech full of good fun. It is impossible that the same country which contains Macdowell's Eve, and Bailey's Eve at the Fountain, can hold Haddock and Spooner. Mr. Punch must avow that he prefers keeping the diviner images, and somehow getting rid of the coarser ones. Pam wanted to know whether the latter would like to stick crinoline on the models, or would be content with African garb. The other Wiscount observed, with more truth than politeness, 'Nude, indeed! I knewed Addock was a Nass.'"

An illustration is appended to the article of a figure resembling a fish in the act of adjusting a crinoline on the Venus de Medici. The crinoline rests upon the shoulders of the statue like a huge extinguisher.

THE CRINOLETTA DISFIGURANS (PUNCH).

AN OLD PARASITE IN A NEW FORM.

By Linley Sambourne ("Punch").

As previously hinted, the crinoletta was only a faint echo of the glories of its earlier prototype. It was a cylindrical contrivance, made up of steels or whalebones, either covered with a series of flounces, or worn underneath the dress like a big bustle. In fact, it began as a bustle, and gradually extended its proportions, wagging and swaying from side to side like the tail of a dragon, as the wearer moved. One well remembers—shall we, indeed, ever forget?—these singular "contraptions" displayed unblushingly in drapers' shops, and even hanging in bundles at the doors.

> "Hang out our banners on the outward walls;
> The cry is still, 'They come.'"

VII
COLLARS AND CUFFS

"*Theodorus.* Have they not also houses to set their ruffes in, to trim them and to trick them, as well as to starch them in?

"*Amphilogus.* Yea, marry have they, for either the same starching houses do serve the turn, or else they have their other chambers and secret closets to the same use, wherein they tricke up these cartwheeles of the divels charet of pride, leading the direct way to the dungeon of hell."

STUBBES, *Anatomy of Abuses.*

VII

COLLARS AND CUFFS

It is to be understood that the terms "collar" and "cuff" are here only intended to refer to those of linen, lace, or similar material, which are more or less separate from the rest of the costume. A "collar" is simply a neck-band, and may be of any material; in the case of Gurth, "born thrall of Cedric the Saxon," it was of iron, and was the symbol of his servitude. The term "collar" is also applied to certain articles of jewellery —

> "The collar of some order, which our King
> Hath newly founded, all for thee, my soul."
>
> Tennyson, Last Tournament.

Collars are of a comparatively modern origin, although some form of covering for the neck has been employed from a very early period. The Romans made use of chin-cloths for the protection of the neck and throat, which were termed "focalia." These were worn by public orators, who from professional considerations were fearful of taking cold, and who, doubtless, contributed in no small degree to render the fashion of chin-cloths general. Some, says a writer on Roman antiquities (the Rev. Father Adam), made use of a handkerchief (sudarium) for this purpose. This is probably the origin of the cravat, which is in many countries called neck-handkerchief.

The thorax, of otter's skin, worn by Charlemagne during the colder months, has already been referred to in a previous chat.

The wimple, also, which was a development of the Roman chin-cloth, and which was worn for such an extended period from the Norman Conquest onwards, is noticed under head-coverings.

During the greater part of the period of York and Lancaster necks were worn bare, the "camise" appearing at the V-shaped junction of the bodice, the neck being ornamented with jewellery.

Shirt-bands were originally connected with neck-ruffs, and the ornament adjoined to the wristband of the shirt was known by the denomination of "ruffle," and was originally called the hand-ruff. In the inventory of apparel belonging to Henry VIII. occurs the item, "4 shirts with bands of silver and ruffles to the same, whereof one is perled with gold."

HENRIETTA, MARQUISE D'ENTRAGUES.

Engraved by Wierix.

The ruff is said to have been first invented in the reign of Henry VI. by a Spanish lady of quality, to hide a wen which grew upon her neck. Its first appearance in England was about the time of the marriage of Queen Mary with Philip of Spain, these personages being represented upon the Great Seal of England in 1554 with small ruffs on the necks and wrists. The ruff appears in none of the portraits by Holbein, with the exception of one at Antwerp, which is dated 1543, the year before the painter's death, and is, moreover, a doubtful work. In many portraits by this master, however, the lawn or cambric shirt appears at the neck with the edges ruffled, and often delicately embroidered. In the well-known portrait of the Duchess of Milan belonging to the Duke of Norfolk, and at present in the National Gallery, such a ruffle appears at the neck and also at the wrists, the edges emphasised by a narrow embroidered border in black silk. This black embroidering was very generally employed during the reign of Henry VIII. It appears in a number of Holbein's portraits, both at the wrists and at the neck, and is quite probably due to Holbein's influence. There can be no reasonable doubt that this great painter influenced the dress of his time. The influence of his artistic personality would be considerable, and it is known that he designed dresses for the ladies of the court, several drawings for which are in the Basle Museum. In the inventory of the apparel of Henry VIII. appears: "One payer of sleves, passed over the arms with gold and silver, quilted with black silk, and ruffled at the hand with strawberry leaves and flowers of gold, embroidered with black silk."

HENRY IV. OF FRANCE.

From an engraving by Goltzius.

Starching at this period had not reached England; ruffs, therefore, must have been an expensive luxury, as the starched linen, imported from Flanders, could not be worn after being washed.

In 1564, one Madame Dinghen, who, as her name suggests, hailed from Flanders, set up as a clear starcher in London, and appears to have made the trade of clear starching an extremely lucrative one. Her terms were four or five pounds for teaching "the most curious wives"[17] to starch, and one pound for the art of seething starch. The "curious wives" subsequently made themselves ruffs of lawn; whereupon arose the general scoffing by-word that they would shortly make their ruffs of spider's web.

A certain Richard Young, described as a justice, for a long time held the monopoly of the manufacture of starch in this country. From the Elizabethan State Papers we learn that in 1589 there was a prosecution against an infringer of the patent, to wit, Charles Glead, a gentleman of Kent, who declared to the Queen's messengers that he would make starch in the face of any patent or warrant yet granted, unless set down by Act of Parliament.

Setting-sticks, strutts, and poking-sticks were the tools used in the process of starching; the first made of wood or bone, and the latter of iron, which was heated in the fire. It was this heated tool which produced that beautiful regularity characteristic of this article of attire.

"They be made of yron or steele, and some of brass kept as bright as silver, yea, and some of silver itselfe; and it is well if in processe of time they grow not to be gold. The fashion whereafter they be made, I cannot resemble to anything so well as to a squirt, or a squibbe, which little children used, to squirt out water withall; and when they come to starching and setting of their ruffes, then must this instrument be heated in the fire, the better to stiffen the ruffe ... and if you woulde know the name of this goodly toole, forsooth, the devill hath given it to name a putter, or else a putting sticke, as I heare say" (Stubbes, "Anatomy of Abuses").

Upon the introduction of these tools, together with starch, ruffs rapidly increased in their proportions.

"They became," says Stow, "intolerably large," and were known in London as the "French fashion," in Paris as the "English monster." The greatest gallant was he who possessed the longest rapier and the deepest ruff. It became necessary to apply one of the usual remedies against these and other extravagances of dress—a proclamation, or an Act of Parliament; in this instance a proclamation. Citizens were compelled to reduce their rapiers to a yard in length and their ruffs to "a nail of a yard" in depth.

The unfinished engraving of the Infanta Isabella Clara Eugenia, Archduchess of Austria,[18] will serve to give a very good idea of the dimensions and general

[17] Stow.

[18] This lady, in 1601, registered a vow not to change her linen until the town of Ostend was taken. The siege lasted three years and three months, by which time her under-clothing had attained a colour which is perhaps easier to imagine than to describe. It provided a name for a stuff, "Couleur Isabella," which was fashionable in France for over a century.

appearance of these articles of attire.

THE INFANTA ISABELLA CLARA EUGENIA.

Engraved by Jan Muller.

Thus friend Philip Stubbes:—"They have now newly found out a more monstrous kind of ruff, of twelve, yea, sixteen lengths apiece, set three or four times double, and it is of some, fitly called, 'three steps and an half to the gallows.'"

The "divells cartwheele" attained its greatest circumference in 1582, when that love of change, inherent in the feminine breast, or possibly the grave and reverend appearance of the ruff, occasioned a revolt amongst the younger women, who were disinclined to hide the beauties of their swan-like necks and throats. The ruff was therefore opened in front and elevated behind. This was the gorget or whisk, which was used both plain and laced.

A curious advertisement appears in the *Mercurius Publicus*, of May 8, 1662:—

"A cambric whisk, with Flanders lace, about a quarter of a yard broad, and a lace turning up about an inch broad, with a stock in the neck and strap hangers down before, was lost between New Palace and Whitehall. Reward, twenty shillings."

These whisks appear to have had a special proclivity for getting lost. Planché ("Cyclopedia of Costume") gives a similar advertisement:—

"'Lost, a tiffany whisk, with a great lace down and a little one up, large flowers, with a rail for the head and peak' (*The Newes*, June 20, 1664)."

On account of the weight of the "whisk"—it was formed of a wire framework covered with point lace—the "piccadilly" or stiffened collar was devised.

Hone in his "Everyday Book" writes—

"The picadil was the round hem, or the piece set about the edge or skirt of a garment, whether at top or bottom; also a kind of stiff collar, made in fashion of a band, that went about the neck and round about the shoulders: hence the term 'wooden picadilloes' (meaning the pillory) in Hudibras. At the time that ruffs and picadils were much in fashion, there was a celebrated ordinary near St. James's, called Piccadilly, because, as some say, it was the outmost or skirt house, situate at the end of the town; but it more probably took its name from one Higgins, a tailor, who made a fortune by picadils, and built this with a few adjoining houses. The name has by a few been derived from a much frequented house for the sale of these articles; but this probably took its rise from the circumstance of Higgins having built houses there, which, however, were not for selling ruffs."

Picardil is the diminutive of "picca," a pike or spear head, and was given to this article of attire from the resemblance of its stiffened edges to the points of spears. Philips ("World of Words," 1693) defines pickardil as the "hem about the skirt of a garment—the extremity or utmost end of everything." Whether the collar gave the name to the district or the district to the collar is a matter of some uncertainty; probably, however, the former. The thoroughfare which we now know as Piccadilly certainly did not exist at the time the picadil was first worn, and the district was then "the utmost end of everything"—that is, beyond the confines of the town.

Piccadilly as a place, or thoroughfare, is mentioned in "The Rehearsal," by George Villiers, second Duke of Buckingham, produced in the winter of 1671:—

> "His servants he into the country sent,
> And he himself to Piccadillé went."

A pickadil is mentioned in the old comedy of "Northward Ho" as part of a woman's dress.

On the visit of James I. to Cambridge in 1615, the Vice-Chancellor of the University thought fit to issue an order prohibiting "the fearful enormity and excess of apparel seen in all degrees, as, namely, *strange piccadilloes*, vast bands, huge cuffs, shoe-roses, tufts, locks and tops of hair, unbeseeming that modesty and carriage of students in so renowned a university."

The Church was still more fierce in its denunciation of these articles of attire. Hall, Bishop of Exeter, in a sermon, after having severely censured ruffs, farthingales, feathers, and paint, concludes with these words, which more than equal anything in Stubbes: "Hear this, ye popinjays of our time: hear this, ye plaster-faced Jezabels: God will one day wash them with fire and with brimstone."

SON OF THE PAINTER DIRCK DE VRIES.

Engraved by Goltzius.

There appears to be considerable contradiction of terms, as applied to the different collars, both with the writers of the time and with subsequent writers. Barnabe Rich, in his "Honesty of the Age," says: "The body is still pampered up in the very dropsy of excess.... He that some forty years sithence should have asked after a pickadilly, I wonder who should have understood him or could have told what a pickadilly had been, either fish or flesh."

There was, however, the small ruff, such as is seen in the portraits of Sir Thomas Gresham and Philip II. of Spain (pp. 121-123). There was the large formal ruff which appears in the portrait of Lord Burleigh (p. 93), and the still larger ruff of the Infanta Isabella Clara Eugenia (p. 187). There was the less formal ruff which fell upon the shoulders, which is seen in many portraits by Franz Hals. There was the high standing pointed collar, such as appears in William Rogers's print of Queen Elizabeth. There was a plain high-standing collar without lace, which went round the back of the head. There was the plain collar of the Cromwellians, which covered the shoulders, and there was also the rich lace collar of the latter part of the reign of Charles I. The plaits of the ruff were occasionally pinned, the rows being sometimes two and three deep. In the "Antiquary," a comedy by Shakerley Marmion, 1641, quoted by Strutt, a lover says to his mistress: "Do you not remember what tasks you were wont to put upon me when I bestowed you gowns and petticoats: and you in return gave me bracelets and shoe-ties? How you fool'd me, and set me sometimes to pin pleats in your ruff two hours together?"

CHARLES I. (IN THREE VIEWS).

After Vandyck. Engraved by W. Sharp.

In an old play called "Lingua; or, the Combat of the Tongue and the Five Senses for Superiority," 1607, one of the characters remarks: —

"It is five hours ago since I set a dozen maids to attire a boy like a nice gentle-woman; but there is such doing with their looking-glasses; pinning, unpinning, setting, unsetting, formings and conformings; painting of blue veins, and rosy cheeks; such a stir with combs, cascanets, purls, falls, squares, busks, bodices, scarfs, necklaces, carkonels, rabatoes, borders, tires, fans, palisadoes, puffs, ruffs, cuffs, muffs, pustles, fusles, partlets, frislets, bandlets, fillets, corslets, pendulets, amulets, annulets, bracelets, and so many lets that the poor lady of the toilet is scarce dressed to the girdle. And now there is such calling for fardingales, kirtles, busk-points, shoe-ties and the like, that seven pedlars' shops, nay, all Stourbridge fair, will scarcely furnish. A ship is sooner rigged by far than a nice gentlewoman made ready."

Towards the latter part of the reign of Charles I. both ruff and whisk give place to the falling band, which was worn both plain and laced. It had, indeed, appeared earlier, even in the latter years of Elizabeth, but was not in general use until the time of Charles. The trouble occasioned by the ruff and whisk appears to have been a factor of their downfall. A character in the "Malecontent," 1604, exclaims: "There is such a deal of pinning these ruffles when a fine cleane *fall* is worth all."

The cravat, or neckcloth, which succeeded the ruff and band, did not come into general use until the latter part of the reign of the Merry Monarch; indeed, some similar form of neck covering became a necessity, on account of the monstrous size of the periwigs. It formed a large bow at the chin, with the ends richly laced. There was a variety of the neckcloth which was twisted like a corkscrew, the ends being drawn through a ring. This was called a "Steinkirk," from the circumstance of the French officers at the battle of that name in 1692, who could not find time to arrange their cravats, and adopted the readier means of twisting them in a knot. The laced ends of the cravat afterwards increased in size, and were drawn through the button-hole of the waistcoat.

"One of the knots of his tye hanging down his left shoulder, and his fringed cravat nicely twisted down his breast, and thrust through his gold button-hole, which looked exactly like my little Barbet's head in his gold collar" (David Garrick, "Bon Ton; or, High Life Below Stairs," 1775).

From a singular little pocket-manual upon the art of tying the cravat, by H. Le Blanc, Esq., published in 1828, it would appear that there are no less than two-and-thirty different styles of tying the cravat. These are demonstrated in sixteen lessons, with illustrations, together with portrait of the author, figured, as a matter of course, in an irreproachable cravat.

"When a man of rank makes his *entrée* into a circle distinguished for taste and elegance, and the usual compliments have passed on both sides, he will discover that his coat will attract only a slight degree of attention, but that the most critical and scrutinising examination will be made on the *set* of his Cravat. Should this unfortunately not be correctly and elegantly put on—no further notice will be taken of him; whether his coat be of the reigning fashion or not will be unnoticed by the assembly—all eyes will be occupied in examining the folds of the fatal Cravat.

"His reception will in the future be cold, and no one will move on his entrance;

but if his Cravat is *savamment* and elegantly formed—although his coat may not be of the last *cut*—every one will rise to receive him with the most distinguished marks of respect, will cheerfully resign their seats to him, and the delighted eyes of all will be fixed on that part of his person which separates the shoulders from the chin—let him speak down-right nonsense he will be applauded to the skies; it will be said—'This man has critically and deeply studied the thirty-two lessons on the Art of Tying the Cravat.' But again reverse the picture—it will be found that the unfortunate individual who is not aware of the existence of this justly celebrated work—however well informed he may be on other subjects—will be considered as an ignorant pretender, and will be compelled to suffer the impertinence of the fop, who will treat him with disdain, merely because his Cravat is not correctly disposed—he will moreover be obliged to hear in silence, and to approve (under pain of being considered unacquainted with the common rules of politeness) all the remarks which he will thus subject himself to—occasionally relieved by hearing a whisper of, 'He cannot even put on a Cravat properly.'"

The reader will not expect, possibly will experience little desire, to be taken through the whole of the two-and-thirty lessons in the art of tying the cravat; a single illustration will probably suffice. It shall be, however, "the sovereign of cravat ties, the 'Nœud Gordien,' the origin of which is lost in the obscurity of antiquity."

The discovery of the name of the brilliant genius to whom the honour of this invention is due has, apparently, defied the most laborious researches on the part of the author. He can only tell us (what he believes is generally known) that Alexander the Great, although he could conquer a whole world, and, like a youthful character in the works of the immortal Dickens, *sigh for more* (soup, however, in the case of the juvenile), was still unable to comprehend the theory of its construction, and adopted the shorter and easier method of cutting it with his sword.

"Attention!"

Cravats when sent from the laundress should undergo a careful examination as to the washing, ironing, and folding, as the set of the cravat and neatness of the tie *entirely depends upon this*. Whether it be plain or coloured is apparently of little moment, and does not in the least affect its formation, but a stout one is recommended as offering more facilities to the daring fingers of the tyro who would accomplish this *chef-d'œuvre*.

It now becomes necessary to meditate deeply and seriously upon the five following directions:—

1. Having carefully chosen the cravat, it must be placed on the neck, the ends left hanging (first time).

2. Take point K, pass it on the inside of point Z, and raise it (second time).

3. Lower point K on the tie, now half formed O (third time).

4. Then, without leaving point K, bend it inside and draw it between the point Z, which you repass to the left Y; in the tie now formed, Y O, thus accomplishing the formation of the knot.

5. "And last." Having accomplished the knot, flattened it with thumb and

fore-finger, or with the iron (a small iron is recommended, with a handle, made expressly for the purpose, and moderately warm), you lower the points K Z, cross them, place a pin at the point of junction H, at once solving the problem which defied the greatest of the world's conquerors.

"The slightest error in the first fold of this tie will render all succeeding efforts, with the same handkerchief, entirely useless — we have said it."[19]

Although, as previously intimated, it is not proposed to wander through the labyrinth of the whole of the two-and-thirty lessons, two others may with advantage be referred to. Our author, though somewhat facetious, is distinctly entertaining.

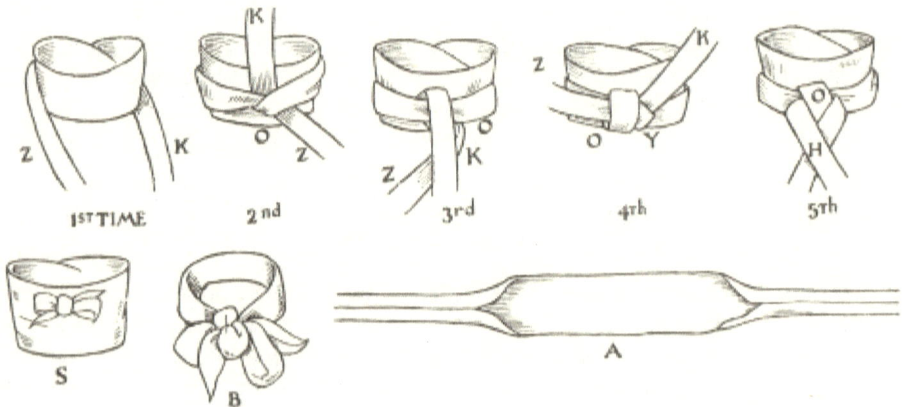

DIAGRAMS ILLUSTRATING THE TYING OF THE "NŒUD GORDIEN."
(CRAVATS)

A. The Cravat folded. B. The Cravat à la Byron. S. The Cravat Sentimentale.

"The Cravat Sentimentale."

This, as its name implies, should only be adopted by those whose physiognomy inspires the tender passion. It may be worn from the age of "seventeen to twenty-seven; after that age it cannot, with propriety, be patronised even by the most agreeable."

"You, then, whom Nature has not gifted with eyes of fire — with complexions rivalling the rose and lily; you, to whom she has denied pearly teeth and coral lips — a gift which, in our opinion, would be somewhat inconvenient; you, in fact, whose faces do not possess that sympathetic charm which, in a moment — at a glance — spreads confusion o'er the senses," &c., pause before adopting the cravat sentimentale — avoid it, in fact; leave it to more highly favoured mortals.

"The Cravat à la Byron."

This must be worn by none but those who would mount the topmost slopes of Parnassus, and drink deeply of the Castalian spring.[20] Our author does not,

[19] "What I have said, I have said" (the Right Hon. Joseph Chamberlain).
[20] The Castalian spring is at the *foot* of the mountain, but it should have been at the

indeed, say so, but the fact is sufficiently evident.

It is universally allowed that the least constraint on the body has a corresponding effect on the mind; a tight cravat, therefore, will "cramp the imagination and, as it were, suffocate the thoughts." This is the reason why Lord Byron submitted to the inconveniences of a cravat, only "when accommodating himself to the *bienséances* of society," and explains the fact that "whenever he is painted in the ardour of composition his neck is always free from the trammels of the neckcloth."

Black silk cravats, at the time of our author's writing (1828), were generally worn, and coloured silk handkerchiefs occasionally patronised. It appears that Napoleon invariably wore a black silk cravat, but at Waterloo it was observed that, contrary to his usual custom, he wore a white neckerchief with a flowing bow, although the day previous he appeared in his black cravat. The superstitiously inclined will note this fact; it is, however, extremely unlikely that the change influenced in the slightest degree the result of the battle.

In the late thirties and early forties Dame Fashion turned her attention in the direction of embroidered muslin. Delicate floral patterns, often displaying considerable taste in design and a high degree of technical skill, were wrought upon collarettes, cuffs, chemisettes, &c.; it was chiefly produced in the north of Ireland, and an extensive trade arose, finding employment for large numbers of women and girls in the counties of Donegal, Tyrone, and Down. The delicacy of the material and the absence of colour, lent itself insensibly to a naturalistic treatment.

As is usual with the caprices of fashion, the art only lasted for a comparatively brief period. It still survives, however, in the form of embroidered handkerchiefs, for which there is even now a demand.

---

top, where the tired and thirsty traveller would be most likely to need it. Besides, it is not to be expected that we could reverse the order of the paragraph—"*we have said it.*"

VIII
HATS, CAPS, AND BONNETS

"'In *that* direction,' the Cat said, waving his right paw round,
'lives a Hatter; and in *that* direction,' waving the other paw, 'lives
a March Hare. Visit either you like; they're both mad.'"

Alice's Adventures in Wonderland.

HEADING: FOOLS IN A MORRIS DANCE.

Bodleian MS. (free rendering).

VIII

HATS, CAPS, AND BONNETS

Mad as a hatter? How comes an honest craft to be thus maligned? Hatters were never mad—that is, not more so than the rest of us—until they adopted the pot of the chimney as a model.[21]

Nature has provided in the hair a natural covering for the head. Hats are not really a necessity.

Dr. Jaeger ("Health Culture") discusses the probable reasons for the greater prevalence of baldness among men than among women. While rejecting the theory that the competition of the beard is precarious to the hair of the head, abstracting from the latter its due nourishment, and pointing out that the long beards and luxuriant heads of hair of our ancestors refute this theory that the more strenuous head-work which falls to the share of the male sex is responsible for the loss of hair; that the unnatural custom of cutting men's hair, first adopted when nature was abandoned in favour of the fashions of civilisation, is to blame for it; that drink, dissolute habits, or heredity is the cause—he finds that a far more probable cause is the difference between the male and female head-covering, "which latter is, as a rule, lighter, more airy, and more porous than the usually almost waterproof and exceedingly absurd male head-coverings, such as the stiff felt hats, and high hats, with the strip of leather which encircles the forehead and effectually retains the perspiration."

"The best head-covering would certainly be—none at all. But usage, and in many cases weather conditions, render this impracticable."... "Not only are the hard hats, now in such general use, injurious on account of the pores of the material being closed, impeding the passage of the exhalation from the head; but the shellac used in stiffening them has an injurious effect, from which the cherry gum

---

[21] It would appear to be a corruption of "mad as an atter (adder)". The word "adder" is *atter* in Saxon, *natter* in German. Its origin, however, is apparently somewhat obscure.

used in the case of the soft hats is comparatively free." He adds: "Of course, soft hats cannot be worn in all cases—on ceremonial occasions the hard hat may be chosen; but ordinarily the hygienically superior soft hat should be worn." Why, however, on occasions of ceremony? Was ceremonial non-existent before the advent of the nineteenth century? It would rather appear that if the nineteenth century is conspicuous for anything it is for its *absence* of ceremonial. There is absolutely no reason why a hat of a particular density, or even of a particular shape, should be necessary to occasions of high ceremonial. Moreover, in this connection it may be very pertinently asked, Is artistic invention so utterly dead that it cannot devise a head-gear which shall fit in with its surroundings on such occasions as call for more dignity and impressiveness in the matter of costume? It is, however, an incontrovertible fact, as a well-known present-day writer has pointed out, that "revolutions are practicable in everything—in manners, morals, government, even religion—sooner than in clothes; and that sumptuary laws are the only laws that have always failed of being obeyed." It is universally admitted that modern dress is intolerably ugly; that it fails, not only upon its artistic side, but also upon the score of utility; yet every suggestion for its improvement is always met by a flat *non possumus*.

MRS. ANNE WARREN (AFTER ROMNEY).

After Romney.

Some form of hood was, doubtless, the earliest covering for the head, either as a separately made-up article, or, as in the case of the Greeks and Romans, formed by the drawing of the pallium or toga over the head to serve as protection during inclement weather. The Romans had a hooded cloak (cucullus) which was worn by the commoner people, and which, in some form or another, has been in use during all subsequent periods. It is, in fact, generally worn at the present day in most parts of the Continent of Europe, and forms an extremely reasonable and convenient article of attire.

The hood formed the principal covering for the head of both sexes during the twelfth, thirteenth, and part of the fourteenth centuries. The hood (chaperon) was a separate article of dress as distinct from the cowl (capuchon), which was attached to and formed part of the cloak or other article of dress, although the two terms are indiscriminately used by the earlier writers.

The hood assumed, in the first instance, more or less the form of the Phrygian cap. The tippet, or tail, was afterwards developed to a considerable length, in the thirteenth century reaching almost to the ground. Dante is usually represented in such a hood, with long tippet, and in the portrait of Cimabue by Simon Memmi, *c.* 1300, the painter appears wearing a hood with a tippet reaching a little below the middle.

The cap or hood worn by "fools" was simply the hood of the fashion of the particular period, with the addition of the cock's comb, the pair of ass's ears and the bells, occasionally worn all together, and often parti-coloured.

HUNTING HAT ORCAGNA, CAMPO SANTO, PISA.

Orcagna, Campo Santa, Pisa.

In the wardrobe accounts of Henry VIII. occurs—"Item, for making a doublet of worsted, lined with canvass and cotton, for William Som'ar, our fool; item, for making of a coat and cap of green cloth fringed with red crule and lined with frize for our said fool."

The men's turbaned head-dress of the reign of Richard II. and later is sufficiently remarkable to warrant a description. It was a long cloth, wound round and round the head—the edges cut, clipped and jagged in various ways—one end of which either stood up on the top of the head or was allowed to fall over the side of the turban, the other end hanging down in front of the body, longer or shorter according to the fancy or caprice of the wearer, the whole presenting a very fantastic appearance, occasionally, however, not ungraceful.

The beginning of this head-dress was simply a different way of wearing the hood, as Mr. Planché has shown by means of two diagrams in his "Encylopedia of Costume." It occurred to some ingenious soul to insert his head in the oval opening in the hood made for the face, to gather up in the form of a fan the portion which covered the shoulders, and to bind it in position by winding the long tippet round the head and tucking in the end of it. Later, no doubt, the head-dress was formally made up by the hatter or tailor, as the case may be, and assumed a more complex character.

HUNTING HAT (IBID.).

Orcagna, Campo Santa, Pisa.

The Greeks, when travelling, protected their heads from the heat or the wet by means of a flat broad-brimmed hat, tied underneath the chin, and allowed to hang on the back when not required on the head. This fashion or device was continued during the Middle Ages, and the hat was often worn over the hood (although this would seem a superfluity), the strings were secured at the breast by means of a moveable ring, which, by being moved up underneath the chin, kept the hat in its place on the head. Such a hat was figured on the wall of the old Palace at Westminster, and has been published in the "Vetusta Monumenta" of the Society of Antiquaries.

During the greater part of the Norman and Plantagenet period the *wimple* or neck-cloth was common. It was a development of the Anglo-Saxon veil or head-cloth (couvre-chef), and an echo of the mailed coif of the period. It is thus referred to by John de Meun: "Par Dieu! I have often thought in my heart, when I have seen a lady so closely tied up, that her neck-cloth was nailed to her chin, or that she had the pins hooked into her flesh."

FIGURE WITH LONG NET-CAUL (G. W. RHEAD).

Such a wimple is figured from Orcagna (Campo Santo, Pisa) on the opposite page (page 120).

The golden net-caul (crestine, creton, crespine, crespinette) appeared during the reigns of Henry III. and Edward I., worn either with or without the wimple and veil, and lasted, in its varying forms, well into the sixteenth century. It either enclosed the hair as within a bag or pouch, or assumed the form of a netted cap, as in the so-called "Beatrice d'Este," attributed to Leonardo da Vinci in the Brera at Milan; or the net-bag above alluded to was elongated so as to form a long pigtail, tied at intervals, often extending almost to the feet, as in the marriage scene in the fresco by Pinturicchio in the Piccolomini Library at Siena. It was often richly ornamented with jewels—

> "Their heads were dight well withal,
> Everich had on a jolyf coronal
> With sixty gems and mo."

This, however, refers to the chaplet or garland commonly worn by the ladies of the fourteenth century.

> "Thenne was I war of a wommon wonderliche clothed,
> Purfylet with pelure the ricchest uppon eorthe,
> I-crouned with a coroune, the King hath no bettre;
> Alle hir fyve fyngres weore frettet with rynges,
> Of the preciousest perre, that prince wered evere;
> In Red Scarlet her Rod i-rybaunt with gold;
> Ther nis no Qweene qweyntore, that quik is alyve."

Piers Plowman, Description of Meed (Bribery).

FROM HAT, FRA ANGELICO, FLORENCE.

The hair was now wound up on either side of the head, the coils either worn without any covering or enclosed within a caul; the veil or curtain being extended at the sides. This marked the commencement of those horned head-dresses which were speedily developed to such an extravagant degree, and so excited the wrath of the satirists of the time.

John de Meun, who completed "The Romaunt of the Rose," observes that these horns appear to be designed to wound the men, and adds: "I know not whether they call gibbets or corbels that which sustains their horns, which they consider so fine, but I venture to say that St. Elizabeth is not in Paradise for having carried such baubles."

FROM HAT, FRA ANGELICO, FLORENCE.

In a volume entitled "Jougleurs et Trouvères," by M. Jubinal, is a satire on horned head-dresses, under the title of "Des Cornetes," from a MS. in the Bibliothèque Royale at Paris, of the beginning of the fourteenth century. In this poem it appears that the Bishop of Paris had preached a sermon directed against extravagance in women's dress, their horns and the bareness of their necks. "If we do not get out of the way of the women we shall be killed; for they carry horns with which to kill men."

This same sermon is quaintly referred to by the Knight of la Tour-Landry in his advice to his daughters: "He said that the women that were so horned were lyche to be horned snails and hertis and unicornes." "I doute that the develle sitte not betwene her hornes, and that he make hem bowe doun the hede for ferde of the holy water." Also the good knight told how there was "onis a gentille woman that come to a fest so straungely atyred and queintly arraied to haue the lokes of the pepille, that all that sawe her come ranne towardes her to wonder lik as on a wilde beaste, for she was atyred with highe longe pynnes lyke a jebet, and so she was scorned of alle the company, and saide she bare a galous on her hede."[22]

[22] The above story was told to the knight by a lady of his acquaintance who was an

The preaching in the Middle Ages appears to have been remarkably effective. Monstrelet, in his Chronicles, relates a story of one Thomas Conecte, a preaching friar, who attacked the steeple head-dresses with great zeal and resolution. His eloquence was such that the women flung down their head-dresses in the middle of his sermon and made a bonfire of them within sight of the pulpit. He frequently had an audience of 20,000 people, the men ranging themselves on one side of the pulpit and the women on the other, the latter appearing "like a forest of cedars with their heads reaching to the clouds."

The impression he created was, however, not a lasting one; as soon as his back was turned the horns again began to grow: "The women that, like snails in a fright, had drawn in their horns, shot them out again as soon as the danger was over."

The horn-shaped head-dress appears in no pictorial documents or monuments older than the reign of Henry IV. The heart-shaped head-dress began with a flat pad on the top of the head, with the sides slightly turned up, enclosed in a silken net, which was often jewelled, the hair being worn in coils above the ears, at the back, or hanging down, as the case may be. The sides were then turned up sharply in the shape of a V, and the head-dress heightened. This was developed in a variety of ways.

The steeple head-dress varied in its height—from a matter of 18 inches or less, to 3 feet—in its ornamentation and colour; it was either plain, or decorated with simple bands or ribbons wound crosswise; it varied, however, chiefly in the veiling. There was a veil thrown over the whole, and falling over the sides of the face, or, the veil was attached to the summit of the steeple and allowed either to hang loose, or was looped at some point at the back. There was also a veil which was attached to the lower border of the steeple at its point of contact with the head, and which completely shrouded the head, front and back; there was also the remarkable arrangement of the veil, which was built up on a system of wires, and which was called the "hennin."

A variation of the "hennin" was the "butterfly," in which the steeple which formed the base of the head-dress was reduced to a comparatively short "caul," and the veil extended itself on either side like the wings of an insect; this, in a slightly different form, continued to the Tudor period.

There was also the "balloon" or turban. This, like the heart-shaped head-dress, commenced with a flat pad, like a cake, which in its earlier stage was invariably richly ornamented, offering no particular variety in its form; when it became round, it developed a second roll around the forehead, with bands at intervals, which formed its constructive elements.

---

eye-witness of the event. We give here Caxton's version:—"For her clothyng and araye was different and no thyng lyke to theyr, and therefore she had wel her part beholdyng and lokyng. Thenne said the good ladyes to her, 'My frende, telle ye us, yf it please yow, how ye name that aray that ye have on your heed?' She answerde and saide, 'The galhows aray.' 'God bless us,' said the good lady, 'the name of hit is not faire.'... 'As ferre as I me remembre of it,' continued the knight's informant, 'hit was highe culewed with longe pynnes of sylver uppon her hede, after the makynge and maner of a gybet or galhows, right straunge and merveylous to se.'"

HEART-SHAPED HEAD-DRESS.

HORNED HEAD-DRESS.

Notwithstanding the strictures passed upon these head-dresses by contemporary moralists or purists and by subsequent writers, who simply echo their sentiments without bringing any independent judgment to bear upon the matter, and who often possess no artistic knowledge or even perception, these head-dresses are often extremely piquant and quaint; extravagance there was, doubtless, and even ugliness; but even the high steeple was not out of proportion, as it must be remembered that the gowns and trains were correspondingly long, thus balancing the high tapering steeple. As a matter of fact, the whole dress was in keeping, the high tapering head-dress, the long tapering toes, the close-fitting sleeves (which, however, were occasionally provided with an outer hanging sleeve, also long), forming an *ensemble* which would compare favourably with the dress of any period.

The Tudor period brought about a complete change in the head-dresses of both men and women; as a matter of fact, dress generally of this period assumed a graver character. Horns, hearts, steeples, and butterflies suddenly disappeared, and the head-dress of the ladies of the Court assumed that diamond-shaped form with which we are familiar in the portraits by Holbein, who doubtless materially influenced the costume of this period. It consisted of a cap and coverchief, and sometimes a hood, the coverchief being generally allowed to fall down on the right side. The cap was invariably richly jewelled and embroidered. Good examples may be seen in the drawing of the Lady Vaux at Windsor and the portrait of Jane Seymour at Vienna. It was a dignified, restrained, and exceedingly beautiful head-dress; if any confirmation of this statement were needed, it is to be found in the remarks of the various lay writers on costume, who invariably describe it as harsh and ugly.

An excellent example of the beautiful flat cap or bonnet worn generally during the Tudor period is to be seen in the portrait of William, Duke of Juliers and Cleves, by Aldegrever (p. 6). The cap, in this instance, is tilted to one side of the head, instead of being worn flat on the top; it is jewelled at intervals along the brim, and plumed. The material is most certainly velvet, which is that most generally used by the nobility, but, in 1571, with the view of encouraging English manufactures, it was by Parliament enacted that all persons above the age of six years, except only the nobility and persons of degree, should on Sabbaths and holydays wear caps of wool, of English manufacture. Twenty-six years afterwards this law was repealed.

This flat cap appears in a number of portraits by Holbein, worn both tilted on one side and flat on the top of the head. A cap of this kind might very well be worn by men at the present day, minus, of course, the plume and jewels, without appearing startlingly obtrusive. It could be made in any cloth, and would be a great improvement on the caps which are at present in use. The extreme refinement, however, of the Tudor cap is due to the material, to the quality of the workmanship, and, in the instance of the portrait above-mentioned, to the rich jewels which adorn it.

Similar shaped headgear has, as a matter of fact, been recently adopted by girls, but they are for the most part vulgar productions, indifferently made, and sold cheaply, and afford abundant evidence of the fact that the milliner possessed no artistic knowledge, or even taste, and had not taken the trouble, possibly had not considered it advisable, to refer to fine examples.

FRANCIS BACON.

Engraved by W. Marshall.

The simple flat cap above mentioned was developed in various ways during the Tudor period, both for men and for women; the brim was either divided in two or more parts, or it was doubled, slashed, and puffed in various ways, the puffing being of a different material and colour to the rest of the hat. For women and for the military, large plumes of ostrich feathers were added. Many examples of the latter may be seen in Hans Burgkmair's "Triumphs of Maximilian." In the equestrian portrait of Charles Howard, Earl of Nottingham (p. 23), we get the pot-hat proper (Elizabethan version), differing very little as to shape from that at present in use, but plumed, with three ostrich feathers and three other pointed ones. The horse is similarly plumed. The hat can scarcely be said to be a thing of beauty, even with the addition of its ostrich plume, and adds nothing to the decorative beauty of the plate, but rather detracts from it.

THOMAS KILLEGREW.

Engraved by William Faithorne.

The centenary of the modern pot-hat was celebrated in Paris only last year, and, amid much jubilation, a number of caustic remarks were made by Madame Sarah Bernhardt and others on the subject of "man's cylindrical attire."

On looking at the various developments during the century, as illustrated in a well-known weekly magazine, the contour of the pot-hat has changed perhaps less than one might suppose. It has not been a continuous development, but, rather, an oscillation backwards and forwards. In point of fact, a continuous development was impossible without taking leave of the pot-hat altogether; one must either retrace one's steps or start upon a new track, as will be seen by a reference to the accompanying diagrams, which must be considered, be it understood, *merely as diagrams*, and not in any sense as representing the limits of the artist's power of realism.

The scale of decorative development is, like the scale of tones in music, *absolute*. It is the principle upon which Nature herself works, and this principle may be as well illustrated by means of the pot-hat as by anything else, as the principle holds good, and may be applied to any "demned thing," as Mr. Mantalini would say.

THE DEVELOPMENT OF THE CHIMNEY-POT HAT.

We have, then, the two primal, elemental forms to work with, the straight line and the curved. Fig. 1 represents the pot-hat in what may be called its primordial state, in which state it stands in the same relation to headgear generally as did Millbank Prison to architecture; it would not be possible to produce less variety except by reducing its height and making its shape an exact parallelogram. In the next figure, by substituting the curved line for the straight lines of the sides and brim, we get a hint of those delicate and subtle curves for which the pot-hat is famous. In Fig. 4—not to weary the gentle reader with a long dissertation, he will at once perceive the principle—the degree of curvature is carried as far as is consonant with dignity or propriety; to carry it further would be to border upon buffoonery; such vagaries could not by any possibility be entertained in a work of such gravity and seriousness as the present. The same may be said of development in the direction of *height*. It only remains to develop the hat by means of reducing the width of its crown at the top, since the dimension AA is absolute, as the article must conform itself to the human cranium, which for present purposes is a fixed quantity. It is at this point that we take an affectionate and regretful leave of the pot-hat proper. Fig. 5 represents the high-crowned hat of the reign of James I., and which, in fact, was worn during the greater part of the Stuart period. "I send you," writes the King (James I.) to his son, in 1623, "for youre wearing, the three bretheren that ye knowe full well, but newlie sette, and the mirroure of Fraunce, the fellow of the Portugall dyamont, quiche I wolde wishe you to weare alone in your hatte, with a little blakke feather"; and to Buckingham he says, "As to thee, my sweete gossippe, I send thee a faire table dyamont, quiche I wolde once have givin thee before if thou wolde have taken it, and I have hung a faire pearle to it for wearing on thy hatte or quhaire thou plaisis, and if my Babie will spaire thee the two long dyamonts in forme of an anker, with the pendant dyamont, it were fit for an admiral to weare…. If my Babie will not spaire the anker from his mistresse, he may well lend thee his rounde broocke to weare, and yett he shall have jewells to weare in his hatte for three great dayes."

ROBERT DEVEREUX, SECOND EARL OF ESSEX.

Engraved by William Rogers.

It was customary to wear jewels either in front of the hat or upon the brim when turned up. Often a single pearl was depended over the edge of the brim. Such a pearl may be seen in William Rogers's portrait of Robert Devereux, second Earl of Essex (Elizabeth's Essex), the hat, in this instance, having a broad brim.

To return to our diagrams. No. 6, a further narrowing of the top of the crown, represents the quaint extinguisher hats which have been worn at various periods, and which are still worn by the Welsh peasantry.

> "There came up a Lass from a country town, intending to live in the City,
> In a steeple-crown Hat and a Paragon Gown, who thought herself won-
> drous pretty;
> Her Petticoat serge, her Stockings were green, her Smock cut out of a
> sheet, Sir;
> And under it all, was seldom yet seen so fair a young maid for the street,
> Sir!"

Roxburghe Ballads, 1685.

By lowering the crown and widening the brim we arrive at the sombrero, No. 7.

The slouch hat turned up on one side, of the Stuart period, was the precursor, historically and decoratively, of the three-cornered hat of the period of the House of Orange. It was afterwards turned up on two sides, and in this stage decorated with feathers, and finally turned up at the back, thus forming the three-cornered hat, which lasted for a century, the feathers disappearing, and the edges trimmed with lace. Such turning up of the brim was called "cocking" the hat.

The different modes of cocking the hat were almost innumerable—in fact, according to the fancy of the wearer; there was the "Monmouth cock," after the unfortunate Duke of that name; the "Ramillie cock," which came in at the Battle of Ramillies in 1706; the military cock and the mercantile cock; and upon the accession of George III. (1760) "a hat worn upon an average six inches and three-fifths broad in the brim, and cocked between Quaker and Kevenhuller."

> "When Anna ruled, and Kevenhuller fought,
> The hat its title from the Hero caught."

Art of Dressing the Hair, 1770.

From a chapter on hats in the *London Chronicle* for 1762 we learn that—"Some wear their hats with the corner that should come over their foreheads high in the air; these are the Gawkies. Others do not above half cover their heads, which is, indeed, owing to the shallowness of their crowns; but, between beaver and eyebrows, expose a blank forehead, which looks like a sandy road in a surveyor's plan.... A gold button and loop to a plain hat distinguishes a person to be a little lunatic; a gold band round it shows the owner to be very dangerously infected; and if a tassel is added, the patient is incurable. A man with a hat larger than common represents the fable of the mountain in labour, and the hats edged round with a gold binding belong to brothers of the turf."

LETITIA BONAPARTE, MOTHER OF NAPOLEON.

With the advent of the French Revolution in 1789 the three-cornered cocked hat disappears, and in 1803 we find a noticeable change in costume. "The French anticipated this invasion by sending over the most unsightly fashions that have ever appeared. The most distinguishing features were the coverings of the head, which consisted, in the one sex of an enormous military cap, and in the other of a bonnet, probably of straw, of a very ungraceful form. They are represented in the accompanying cut, taken from a caricature entitled 'Two of the Wigginses—Tops and Bottoms of 1803,' published on the 2nd of July in that year" (Thomas Wright, "Works of Gillray").

ANNE DAY.

Engraved by James Macardell.

In 1765 a large hood appeared called calash, made of a framework of whale-bone hoops, resembling the hood of a carriage (*calèche*), and pulled over the head by means of a string. It is said to have been introduced into England by the Duchess of Bedford.

"TWO OF THE WIGGINSES — TOPS AND BOTTOMS OF 1803 (GILLRAY)."

Gillray.

What shall we say to the page of Parisian head-dresses from *Bell's Fashionable Magazine* for April, 1812, three years before the Battle of Waterloo?

Goldsmith, in a short essay "on the ladies' passion for levelling all distinction of dress," says: "Foreigners observe that there are no ladies in the world more beautiful or more ill-dressed than those of England. Our countrywomen have been compared to those pictures where the face is the work of a Raphael, but the draperies thrown out by some empty pretender, destitute of taste, and entirely unacquainted with design."

He adds, by way of compensation to the ladies, "If I were a poet I might observe, on this occasion, that so much beauty, set off with all the advantages of dress, would be too powerful an antagonist for the opposite sex; and therefore it was wisely ordered that our ladies should want taste, lest their admirers should entirely want reason."

It has always been, however, and is still, a stock saying with foreigners that English women are ill-dressed, but the saying has little point in it, since the majority of English fashions still come from abroad. On the comparatively rare occasions when English women rely upon their own invention, taste, and judgment, they appear better dressed than the women of any European country. English women under these circumstances, therefore, if the above statement as to their personality be true, must necessarily be the most charming creatures in the world.

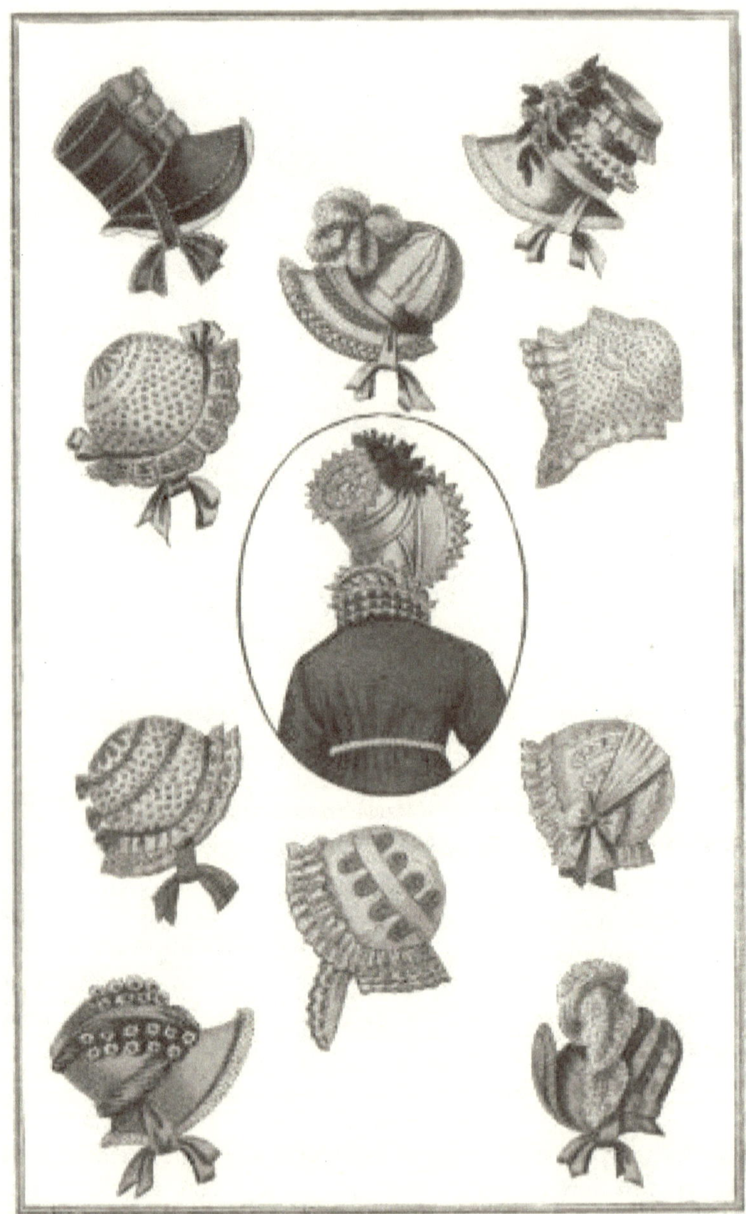

PARISIAN HEAD-DRESSES FOR APRIL, 1812.

Bell's Fashionable Magazine.

Amongst modern head-dresses the Spanish mantilla undoubtedly stands out in pleasant relief from the general rule of the commonplace which obtains at present. It is an entirely becoming head-dress, and reasonable, as is also the habit of Spanish women of carrying fans, which are usually attached to the waist, and serve also the purpose of sunshades, being held up to the head on the sunny side of the street. The action is a most graceful one, and the convenience is obvious.

The panama hat is certainly the most satisfactory male headgear, both as regards appearance, health, durability, and comfort.

The "bowler" can scarcely be said to be a thing of beauty. It has, however, been rendered historic by the Right Honourable John Burns, who has established a precedent by appearing at Buckingham Palace in this form of head-covering for the purpose of receiving his seals of office.

To return once again, and finally, to the chimney-pot. Milan has just recently inaugurated her third International Exposition of Industries, Commerce, and Art:—

"An amusing sidelight of the Exhibition is the unprecedented stimulus to the sale of stovepipe hats occasioned by a rigid regulation excluding every other kind from the inaugural function. Such a rigid enforcement is quite unknown in Rome itself, where there are said to be Cabinet Ministers, Senators, and Deputies who are innocent of ever having donned one. The story is told that several provincial Deputies who were invited to Milan were so fearful of mishap that they bought tall hats *for their wives as well as themselves*" (*Vide* daily paper).

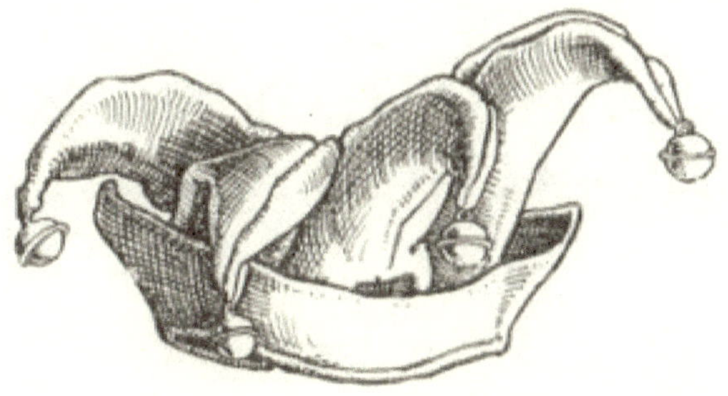

FOOL'S CAP OF LEATHER, GERMAN (S.K.M.).

Worn by the court fool of an Elector of Mayence (seventeenth century).

South Kensington Museum.

IX
THE DRESSING OF THE HAIR, MOUSTACHIOS, AND BEARD

"Truewit. A wise lady will keep guard always upon the place, that she may do things securely. I once followed a rude fellow into a chamber, where the poor madam, for haste, and troubled, snatched at her peruke to cover her baldness, and put it on the wrong way.

"Clerimont. O prodigy!

"Truewit. And the unconscionable knave held her in compliment an hour with that reversed face, when I still looked when she should talk from the other side.

"Clerimont. Why, thou shouldst have relieved her.

"Truewit. No, faith, I let her alone, as we'll let this argument, if you please, and pass to another."

BEN JONSON, The Silent Woman, Act I. sc. 1.

HEADING: COMB (ITALIAN, FOURTEENTH CENTURY).

IX

THE DRESSING OF THE HAIR, MOUSTACHIOS, AND BEARD

There was nothing new, even in the days of Solomon; wigs, curling irons, hair powder, and turned-up moustachios being no exception to the rule.

We have abundant evidence, both from the concurring testimony of authors and from the actual works which have come down to us, that heated irons were employed from a very early period for the purpose of curling the hair and beard. Both with the Assyrians, and the Greeks of the earlier period, the hair and beard were plaited in a series of symmetrical curls and ringlets, displaying the utmost degree of formality in their arrangement.

The hair and beard of Belshazzar when he "made a great feast to a thousand of his lords," and received an intimation of an unpleasant character, conveyed to him in an unusual manner, were certainly curled in such wise, and probably dyed and powdered, as was the custom, the powder, however, being gold instead of flour, as in more recent days. As a matter of fact, gold was employed in various ways as an enrichment to the hair. The Kings of Egypt had their beards interwoven with gold thread.

ASSYRIAN BAS-RELIEF.

Layard's "Nineveh."

Herodotus assures us that the skulls of the Egyptians were much harder than those of the Persians, owing to the national custom of shaving the heads of their children at a very early age. He adds, "In other countries the priests of the gods wear long hair; in Egypt they have it shaved. With other men it is customary in mourning for the nearest relations to have their heads shorn; the Egyptians, on occasions of death, let the hair grow both on the head and face, though till then they used to shave."

The ceremonies and customs relating to the beard are innumerable. The management of the beard formed a considerable part of the religion of the Tartars, who waged a long and bloody war with the Persians, declaring them infidels, though in other respects of the same faith as themselves, because they refused to cast their whiskers after the mode or rite of the Tartars.

It has been recorded that the Greeks wore their beards until the time of Alexander, who, fearful lest the length of their beards should prove a handle to their enemies, commanded the Macedonians to be shaven, and the first who shaved at Athens ever after bore the addition of χορσης (shaven) on medals. Notwithstanding this statement, however, Philip, the father of Alexander, as well as Amyras and Archelous, his predecessors, are represented without beards.

BEARDED BACCHUS (HOPE'S "COSTUME OF THE ANCIENTS").

Hope's "Costume of the Ancients."

According to Pliny, the Romans did not begin to shave until the year of Rome 454, when P. Titinius brought over a stock of barbers from Sicily. Pliny adds that Scipio Africanus was the first to introduce the fashion of shaving daily. It became the custom to have visits of ceremony at the cutting of the beard for the first time. The first fourteen Roman Emperors shaved until the time of the Emperor Adrian, who discontinued the practice and wore a beard, for the purpose, however, of hiding the scars on his face.

From Gregory of Tours we learn that in the Royal family of France it was for a long time the peculiar privilege of Kings and Princes of the blood to wear long hair, artfully dressed and curled; everybody else was polled, as a sign of inferiority and obedience. To cut off the hair of a son of France under the first race of Kings was to exclude him from the right of succession to the crown, and to reduce him to the condition of a subject.

French historians, however, tell us that Charlemagne wore his hair short, his son much shorter, and Charles the Bald, as his surname indicates, none at all.

Good Luitprand furiously declaimed against the Emperor Phocyas for wearing long hair, after the manner of all the other Emperors of the East, with the exception of Theophilus, who, being bald, enjoined all his subjects to shave their heads, like the fox of Æsop, who, having survived the experience of a trap by the sacrifice of his tail, harangued the other foxes on the inconvenience of tails in general, and endeavoured to persuade them to cut off theirs also.

GREEK HEAD-DRESSES (IBID.).

Hope's "Costume of the Ancients."

In the Church, too, in spite of the beard of Aaron, "that went down to the skirts of his garments," the Nazarite law, and the reputed long hair of the founder of Christianity, the priesthood habitually condemned long hair as being inconsistent with the sacred character of the priest's office. Pope Anictus is supposed to have been the first to forbid the clergy to wear long hair. "The Holy Prelate, Wulstan, reproved the wicked of all ranks with great boldness but he rebuked those with the greatest severity who were proud of their long hair."[23] The Nazarite vow is an act of sacrifice in accordance with the terms of the law laid down in Num. vi. 1-21: "All the days of the vow of his separation shall no razor come upon his head"; "He shall be holy, and shall let the locks of his hair grow."

The Nazarite has been regarded as a conqueror who subdued his temptations, and who wore his long hair as a crown, the hair being worn *rough* as a protest against foppery. Another view, however, is that it was kept elaborately dressed, a proof of the existence of the custom being seen in the seven locks of Samson:—

"And she made him sleep upon her knees; and she called for a man, and she caused him to shave off the *seven locks of his head*; and she began to afflict him, and his strength went from him" (Judg. xvi. 19).

Let us listen to the story in the quaint, silvery music of Chaucer:—

> "This Sampson neyther siser dronk ne wyn
> Ne on his heed com rasour noon ne schere
> By precept of the messager divyn
> For alle his strengthes in his heres were.
> *   *   *   *   *
>
> Unto his lemman Dalida he tolde
> That in his heres al his strengthe lay
> And falsly to his foomen sche him solde
> And slepying in hir barm upon a day
> Sche made to clippe or schere his heres away
> And made his foomen al his craft espien
> And whan thay fond him in this array
> Thay bound him fast and put out bothe his yen.
>
> "But er his heer clipped was or i-schave
> Ther was no bond with which men might him bynde
> But now is he in prisoun in a cave
> Ther as thay made him at the querne grynde
> O noble Sampson strengest of al man kynde
> O whilom jugge in glory and in richesse
> Now maystow wepe with thine eyyen blynde
> Sith thou fro wele art falle to wrecchednesse."

Monk's Tale.

While the hair was the pride, the glory, and the strength of Samson, it was the bane of Absalom, for by the abundance of his hair he met his death. "In all Israel there was none to be so much praised as Absalom for his beauty: from the sole of his foot even to the crown of his head there was no blemish in him. And when he polled his head (for it was at every year's end that he polled it: because the hair was heavy, therefore he polled it), he weighed the hair of his head at two hundred

---

[23] William of Malmesbury.

shekels after the king's weight."[24] Had he polled it at more frequent intervals he might have made good his succession to the crown, and Solomon never have been king, for Absalom had "stolen the hearts of the people of Israel."

ROMAN HEAD-DRESSES (IBID.).

Hope's "Costume of the Ancients."

As in a mighty river we may trace back its course to the little rill or rivulet which trickles from the mountain side, so we may often trace the origin of great events to very small beginnings. How might the face of both French and English history have been changed but for Peter Lombard's dislike of a beard! Louis VII. imagined it a matter of conscience to give an example of submission to the command of the bishops on the subject of long hair, and to atone for his many cruelties by being shaved in public. He reckoned, however, without his—wife, Eleanor of Aquitaine, a jocose madcap, who rallied him upon his short hair and shaven chin. "I thought I had married a prince, but find I have wedded nothing but a monk."

---

[24] 2 Sam. xiv. 25, 26.

The breach occasioned by a bare face was widened, and the marriage dissolved. Six weeks afterwards Eleanor was again a wife—Henry, Duke of Normandy, who afterwards reigned as Henry II. of England, being the husband, who obtained with her fair Aquitaine with its three provinces. Hence arose those wars which ravaged France for near three centuries, in which upwards of three millions of Frenchmen perished on the fields of Cressy, Agincourt, and Poitiers, and on many a lesser field.

Henry I. issued an edict for the suppression of long hair, and as a natural consequence long hair immediately became the rage. This edict, however, was the result of a visit to Normandy, and the preaching of a prelate named Serlo, whose eloquence was such that the monarch and his courtiers were moved to tears. The astute priest, perceiving the impression he had created, immediately whipped a pair of scissors from his sleeve and cropped the whole congregation!

The patriarchal beard and long hair of Edward III., as exhibited in his effigy at Westminster, is in strict conformity with the general character of this serious minded monarch, strongly contrasting with the character of his successor, Richard of Bordeaux, who was the greatest fop of the day.

During the century which followed the reign of Edward III. beards were worn of every imaginable cut. There was the fantail beard, with its wadded nightcap for protection during sleep, of the stiffening which was applied. There was, as later, the cathedral beard, the spade beard, the stiletto beard, and there was an extraordinary curled tuft which resembled a corkscrew. There was apparently as much variety of colour as of form—

"I will discharge it in either your straw-colour beard, your orange tawny beard, your purple-in-grain beard, or your French-crown-colour beard, your perfect yellow" ("A Midsummer Night's Dream," Act I. sc. 2).

Our Royal "Bluebeard" registered a solemn vow before the French Ambassador that he would never touch razor till he had visited "his good brother" upon the Field of the Cloth of Gold, the "good brother" making a similar vow. With characteristic "English perfidy" Henry broke his vow, while the Frenchman remained true; it was therefore found necessary for Sir Thomas Boleyn to apologise for his master's bad faith by saying that "the Queen of England felt an insuperable antipathy to a bushy chin."

Henry, indeed, not only shaved his own chin and wore his hair short, but commanded all his subjects to do the same. He granted the barbers a new charter, incorporated them with the surgeons, and became a member of their company.

It was found that the "science and connyng of Physyke and Surgerie" was practised by unskilful persons, "common artificers, as Smythes, wevers, and women,"[25] who "boldely and custumably take upon theim grete curis, and thyngys of great difficultie, in which they partely use socery and whichcrafte" to the grievous

---

[25] "Phisicke is good, and yet I would wish that every ignorant doult, and especially women, that have as much knowledge in phisick or surgery as hath jackeanapes, being but smatterers in the same noble sciences, should be restrained from the publike use therof" unless they do it *gratis* (Stubbes, "Anatomy of Abuses," 1583).

hurt of the Kyng's liege people. It was therefore enacted that none should practise as a physician and surgeon in London except by examination, duly approved by the Bishop of London or Dean of St. Paul's(!). As it seemed needful to provide skilful surgeons for the "helth of mans body whan infirmities and seckness shal happen," and as there are many surgeons in London who give instructions to students, who exercise of the said science "to the greate relief, comforte, and soccour of muche people, and to the sure savegard of their bodily helth, their lymmes and lyves," and as two companies of surgeons exist in London, one "the Barbours of London, and thother company the Surgeons of London," which company of barbours were first incorporated "undre the greate Seale of the late King of famous memory, Edwarde the iiijth, dated at Westminster the xxiiijth day of February in the first yere of his reigne," these two companies ought therefore to be united into one body, with a common seal, power to hold lands, and all the rights of both the old companies.

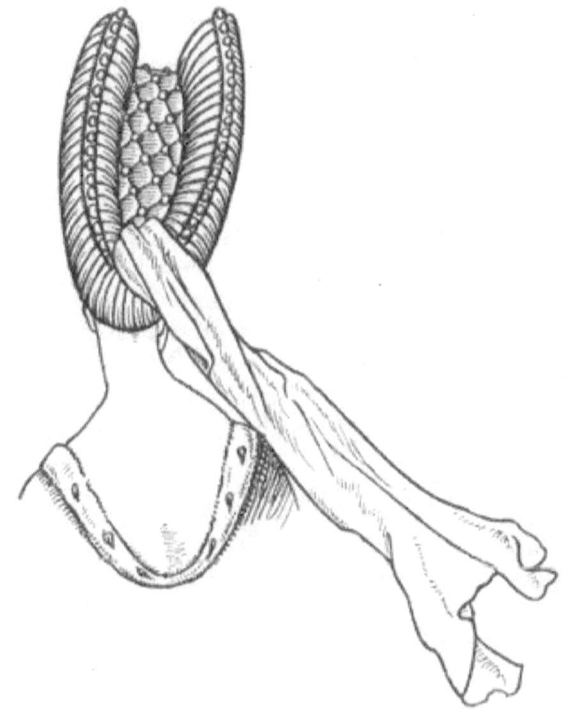

HEAD-DRESS FROM VIOLLET LE DUC (FIFTEENTH CENTURY).

From Viollet le Duc (Fifteenth Century).

It was further found that surgeons were in the habit of taking diseased persons into their houses, where they "doo use and exercise barbery, as wasshing and shaving, and other feates therunto belonging," very perilous to the King's people. Now, "after the feast of the Nativitie of our Lorde God next coming," no barber in London shall practise surgery, "letting of bludde, or any other thing belonging to surgery, *drawing of teth onelye except.*" And no surgeon shall "occupye or exercise the feate or crafte of barbarye or shaving," either by himself or by any other for him, to his or their use.

It was also provided that any person may keep a barber or a surgeon as his servant, who may practise in his master's house.

It would appear that the observance of the Lord's day was more strictly enforced in the seventeenth century than it is at present—

"Att the Councell Chamber on Ouze bridge at York ye xxth of June, A.D. 1676," it was declared and enacted that whereas barber surgeons have been shaving and cutting hair on the Lord's day, We order, that if "any brother of the said company tonse, barbe, or trim any person on the Lord's day, in any Inn," or other place, public or private, of which the Lord Mayor shall judge, he shall be fined ten shillings, and the searchers of the said company for the time being are to make diligent search in all public and private houses as aforesaid, for discovery of such offenders.

1745 was the fatal year of the separation of the barbers from their more dignified colleagues. Their wings were clipped, their privileges curtailed, the barber's pole and basin, however, still remaining, in silent, eloquent testimony of their former glory and greatness.[26]

In the reign of Good Queen Bess the campaign against long hair is continued. Philip Stubbes extols barbers to the skies: "There are no finer fellowes under the Sunne, nor experter in their noble science of barbing than they be." Barbers are necessary. "I cannot but marvell at the beastlinesse of some ruffians (for they are no sober Christians) that will have their hair grow over their faces like monsters, and savage people; rather like mad men than otherwise, hanging downe over their shoulders, as womens haire doth; which indeed is an ornament to them, being given them as a sign of subjection." In man it is a "shame and reproch, as the Apostle proveth."

During the reign of the Stuarts long hair was the vogue—with "love-locks" and "heart breakers."

> "A long love-lock on his left shoulder plight,
> Like to a woman's hair, well showed a woman's sprite."

> "His beard was ruddy hue, and from his head
> A wanton lock itself did down dispread
> Upon his back; to which, while he did live,
> Th' ambiguous name of *Elf-lock* he did give."

The Great Oyer.

The absurd fashion of painting and patching the face, much ridiculed by the satirists, began in the reign of Elizabeth.

> "Whers the Devill?

---

[26] The fillet which encircles the barber's pole indicates the ribbon used for bandaging the arm in bleeding, and the basin the vessel to receive the blood.

He's got a boxe of women's paint—
Where pride is, thers the Divell too."

Quips upon Questions, 1600.

"This is an Embleame for those painted faces,
Where devine beautie rests her for awhile,
Filling their browes with stormes and great disgraces,
That on the pained soule yeelds not a smile,
But puts true love into perpetuall exile;
Hard-hearted Soule, such fortune light on thee
That thou maist be transform'd as well as he."

CHESTER'S Love's Martyr, 1601.

A PAINTED FACE (ROXBURGHE BALLADS).

Roxburghe Ballads.

By the reign of James I. this ridiculous fashion had become common. All sorts of curious devices were made use of—spots, stars, crescents, and in one woodcut a coach and coachman with two horses and postilions appear upon the lady's forehead. The fashion continued for a long period; in fact, during the greater part of the Georgian era, when it had degenerated into mere spots or small patches. At the close of the eighteenth century it had entirely disappeared.[27]

"Wherfor, faire doughtres, takithe ensaumple, and holde it in your herte that ye put no thinge to poppe, painte, and fayre youre visages, the which is made after Goddes ymage, otherwise thanne your Creatoure and nature hath ordeined; and that ye plucke no browes, nother temples, nor forhed; and also that ye wasshe not the here of youre hede in none other thing but in lye and water" ("Advice of the Knight of La Tour Landry to his iij doughtres").

THE INVINCIBLE PRIDE OF WOMEN.

I have a Wife, the more's my care, who like a gaudy peacock goes,
In top-knots, patches, powder'd hair, besides she is the worst of shrows;
This fills my heart with grief and care to think I must this burden bear.

It is her forecast to contrive to rise about the hour of Noon,
And if she's trimm'd and rigg'd by five, why this I count is very soon;
Then goes she to a ball or play, to pass the pleasant night away.

And when she home returns again, conducted by a bully spark,
If that I in the least complain, she does my words and actions mark,
And does likewise my gullet tear, then roars like thunder in the air.

I never had a groat with her, most solemnly I here declare;
Yet she's as proud as Lucifer, and cannot study what to wear:
In sumptuous robes she still appears, while I am forc'd to hide my ears.

The lofty Top-knots on her crown, with which she sails abroad withal,
Makes me with care, alas! look down, as having now no hope at all,
That ever I shall happy be in such a flaunting Wife as she.

In debt with every shop she runs, for to appear in gaudy pride,
And when the milliner she duns, I then am forc'd my head to hide:
Dear friends, this proud imperious wife she makes me weary of my life.

Roxburghe Ballads, circa 1686.

Wigs of various kinds have been in use from very early periods, as the grace and ornament which the hair imparts to the human frame have always been generally recognised. The want of it has ever been deemed a subject of reproach, held in ridicule, in all climes; hence the constant recourse to false hair.

Strutt affirms that the beards of the Egyptians, as well as the coverings for the head, appear to have been made of false hair, and removed when the face was shaved. There is no doubt that the Egyptians wore wigs, as examples are to be seen

[27] "He speaks like a lady for all the world, and never swears, as Mr. Flash does, but wears nice white gloves, and tells me what ribands become my complexion, where to stick my patches, who is the best milliner, where they sell the best tea, and which is the best wash for the face and the best paste for the hands; he is always playing with my fan, and showing his teeth; and when ever I speak, he pats me—so—and cries, 'The devil take me, Miss Biddy, but you'll be my perdition—ha, ha, ha!'" (David Garrick, "Miss in Her Teens," 1747).

in the British and other museums.

The wig given in the illustration is probably a woman's, and was found near the small temple of Isis at Thebes. It belongs to the seventeenth dynasty, about B.C. 1500; it is formed of natural curlings of the hair in the upper portion, and the lower portion, which was originally much longer, consists of long, thin plaits, a number of which have been broken off and decayed, the thin plaitings contrasting very happily with the natural curls.

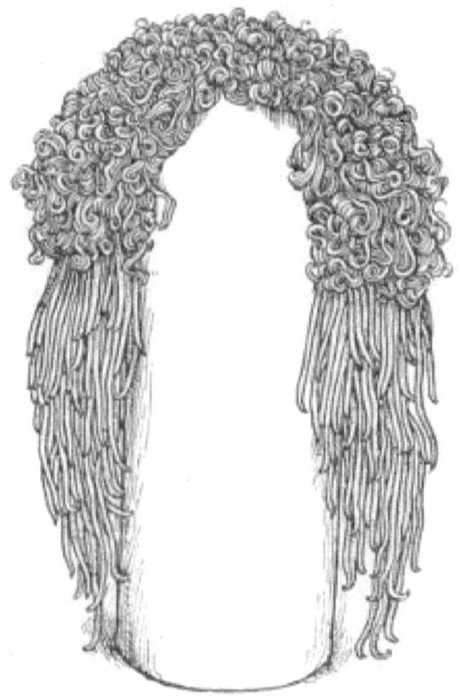

WIG, EGYPTIAN, B.C. 1500 (BRITISH MUSEUM).

British Museum.

Lamprideses describes the wig of the Emperor Commodus as powdered with scrapings of gold, and oiled with glutinous perfumes for the powder to hang by.

Wigs first appear in England during the reign of Stephen, but are seldom mentioned until the Tudor period. The "Maiden Queen" is popularly supposed to have had her head shaved, and to have worn a wig. Mary Queen of Scots had a most complete collection of wigs, and it is recorded that she wore one at her execution.

The periwig first appears in history as the headgear of a fool. In the privy purse expenses of Henry VIII. for December, 1522, occurs the entry: "For a peryke for Sexton the King's fool xx shillings." By the middle of the same century their use had become general, and it was dangerous for children to wander alone, as they were liable to be deprived of their hair for the manufacture of these articles.

The periwig blossomed out during the reign of Charles II., and attained enormous proportions; it was often gaily decked with ribbons and allowed to hang over the front and back for some distance.

The gossiping Pepys, complaining in his diary of October 30, 1663, of his extravagant purchases in wigs, clothes, &c., mentions, amongst other things, two periwigs, "one whereof cost me £3 and the other 40s. I have worn neither yet, but will begin next week, God willing."

> "A Londoner into the country went,
> To visit his tennants, and gather in rent;
> He on a brave gelding did gallantly ride,
> With boots and with spurs, and a sword by his side.
> Because that the Innkeepers they will not score
> He lined his pockets with silver good store;
> And he wore a wigg cost three guineas and more;
> His hat was cockt up, Sir, behind and before."

Roxburghe Ballads, 1688.

Wigs when first worn were extremely expensive, costing as much as a hundred guineas, and their value often led to their being stolen from the head.

The different shapes which the wig assumed were innumerable, and the different classes of society were identified with particular shaped wigs. There were the clerical and the physical; the huge tie peruke for the man of law, the brigadier and the tremendous fox-ear or cluster of temple curls with a pigtail behind, for the Army and Navy. (The Army pigtail was shortened to seven inches in 1804, and in 1808 was cut off altogether.) The merchant, the man of business and of law affected the grave full-bottom; the tradesman was distinguished by the snug bob or natty scratch; the country gent by the natural fly and hunting peruke; "the coachman wore his, as do some to this day, in imitation of the curled hair of a water-dog."

There were also, as a writer in the *London Magazine* of 1753 informs us, the pigeon's wing, the comet, the cauliflower, the royal bird, the staircase, the ladder, the brush, the wild boar's back, the temple, the rhinoceros, the corded wolf's paw, Count Saxe's mode, the she-dragon, the rose, the crutch, the negligent, the chancellor, the cut bob, the long bob, the half natural, the chain-buckle, the corded buckle, the snail back, and many others.

"The Judge," says Fortescue, "while he sitteth in the King's Courts, weareth a white quoife of silke, which is the principal and chiefe insignement of habite wherewith Sergeants-at-lawe are dekked, and neither the Justice nor the Sergeant shall ever put off the quoife, no, not in the King's presence, though he bee in talke with his majestie's highnesse."

The coif-cap is still worn on occasions when the Judge passes sentence of death, but with the colour changed to black, the cap being worn over the wig.

BEAU FIELDING.

After Wissing.

Samuel Rogers in his "Table Talk" tells a good story of Lord Ellenborough's wig. On one occasion when the distinguished Judge was about to go on circuit, his Lady intimated that she would like to accompany him. He replied that he had no objection, provided she did not encumber the carriage with band-boxes, which were his utter abhorrence. During the first day's journey, happening to stretch his legs, he struck his foot against something below the seat, and discovered that it was one of the detested band-boxes. Up went the window, and out went the band-box. The coachman stopped, and the footman, thinking that the band-box had tumbled out of the window by some extraordinary chance, was about to pick it up. "Drive on!" thundered his lordship. The band-box was accordingly left by the ditch. Upon his arrival at the court at which he was to officiate, and array-ing himself for his appearance at the court-house, "Now," said he, "where's my wig?—where *is* my wig?" "My lord," replied the attendant, "it was thrown out of the carriage window!"

PORTRAIT OF THE PAINTER HYACINTHE RIGAUD.

From 1770 onwards" was the period of the highest blossoming of feminine head-gear. The bodies of these enormous creations were formed of tow, over which the hair was drawn in great curls, rolls, bobs, &c., with false hair added, the whole freely plastered over with powder, pomatum, &c., decorated with huge bows, ribbons, feathers, and flowers.

In the "Macaroni Dialogue" — a colloquy between Sir Harry Dimple and Lady Betty Frisky — in the *Lady's Magazine*, iv. 1773, which is illustrated by a picture of a lady and gentleman discussing with great animation the merits of the male and female costumes of this period, in which they are clad, the gentleman is presenting to the lady a nosegay, and she invites his interest in the excessively lofty coiffure which she is wearing.

RIDICULOUS TASTE, OR THE LADY'S ABSURDITY.

"Permit me to present your ladyship with this boquet — it has been to Warren's, doubly perfumed and scented; so that *positively*, my lady, it has not the least of the vulgar odour of the flowers." "I vow, Sir Harry, you are a man of such nice sensations that you would do honour to nobility. I am surprised you have hitherto been overlooked in the creation of Lords." "To be sure, my lady, my taste has never yet been called into question. It was I who first dethroned those abominable monsters the Bucks, and established the reign of the Macaronies—who first improved upon the Poudre à la maréchale by throwing in a dash of the violet. This hat your ladyship sees is of my own cocking—those barbarians the hatters have no more idea of 'de retrousser un chapeau' for a man of genuine taste, than they know how to wear it, and send it home with the smell of the dye, almost sufficient to make one faint. I always order my valet to give it a thorough perfume before it comes into my presence." "O! exquisite refinement—what do you think of my cap?" "Amazing, my lady, beyond description—yet, had it been but an inch higher, it would have been at the very summit of the mode—you would then have been unable to come into a room without stooping, or riding in a coach without the top being heightened." "You see, Sir Harry, I have anticipated you: that upon the table is *two* inches higher; I shall wear it to-morrow night at the Pantheon." "I hope I shall have the felicity of your ladyship's hand to walk a minuet. We shall have all eyes upon us, no doubt!" "I beg, Sir Harry, that your club may be increased in proportion to my head, else we shall not be fit partners." "My lady, I shall have it as large again—my toupee shall be heightened three inches." "You will then, Sir Harry, be the emperor of the Macaronies." "And you, my lady, their empress."

In a print of the period of the French lady in London, by J. H. Grimm, published by Carrington Bowles, who appears to have been somewhat of a wag amongst publishers, devoting himself to the curious and extraordinary, the lady is seen bowing as she enters the room, the head-dress reaching to the top of the ceiling. The good man of the house is so astonished and overcome that he falls to the ground, bringing the table with him. A large picture upon the wall represents the Peak of Teneriffe.

Another print, issued by the same publisher, representing the fashionable head-dresses for the year 1776, shows two ladies out walking, attended by their black servant, with head-dresses two yards high.

In the illustration given of "Ridiculous Taste, or the Lady's Absurdity," Monsieur le Friseur is mounted on a high pair of steps, and is operating upon the summit of the lady's coiffure; a gentleman is taking stock, and giving orders from below.

In the example given from "Jacquemin," the head-dress represents a ship in full sail.

In 1776 an etching appeared entitled "Bunker's Hill, or America's Head-dress." The enormous headgear of the lady represents the battle, with tents, fortifications, cannon, and battalions. From the crests of the three hills of the head-dress, which are duly fortified and defended with soldiery and cannon, three banners are flying, on which are figured, respectively, a goose, a monkey, and two ladies holding arrows. The lower portion of the head-dress represents a sea fight.

THE FRENCH LADY IN LONDON.

In the same year appeared "The New Fashioned Phaeton," a mezzotint representing a conveyance provided with springs, which lifts the lady and her headgear up to the first-floor window, and does away with the need for walking up and down stairs.

Another print issued by the same publisher is a "hint to the ladies to take care of their heads." The ladies' head-dress having caught alight from a chandelier hanging from the ceiling of a high room, and people are putting out the fire by means of large squirts.

HEAD-DRESS (FROM JACQUEMIN).

From Jacquemin.

A charming design for a fancy head-dress is entitled "Betty the Cook maids Head drest." It is in the form of a heart, the centre of which is occupied by a Cheshire cheese with mice, surrounded with a border of greengrocery, &c. On the summit is a stove, with fire alight and meat cooking. A monkey sits upon the stove, wearing a fool's cap and bells, and admiring himself in a mirror. On either side of the head-dress are two trophies composed respectively of a mop and fire-irons and a besom and cooking utensils.

The legend runs—

> "The taste at present all may see,
> But none can tell what is to be.
> Who knows, when fashion's whims are spread,
> But each may wear this kitchen head?
> The noddle that so vastly swells,
> May wear a fool's cap hung with bells."

High plumes of feathers re-appeared in 1796. Gillray produced a caricature of a fashionable belle journeying to the Assembly Rooms at Bath in a sedan chair. The top of the conveyance is opened to accommodate the lady's head-dress, a monstrous feather projecting yards above the sedan—a parasol is fastened to a long pole strapped on the back of the hindermost portion and protecting the top.

During the feather period, a favourite idea was to represent attacks by ostriches, peacocks, and other interested birds. This occurs in a number of prints of the period. The print by John Collet, 1779, of "The Feathered Fair is a Fright; or, Restore the Borrowed Plumes," represents two girls attacked by ostriches:—

> "Two lassies who would like their mistresses shine,
> On their heads clap'd some feathers to make them look fine;
> When two ostriches suddenly came within sight,
> And put the poor girls in a terrible fright.

> "But how the Birds got to England's no matter,
> Tho' they certainly made a most terrible clatter;
> Fanny screamed as she ran, and scampering Polly,
> With her Fan fought the birds in defence of her folly."

If the reader be curious in regard to the *modus operandi* of these astonishing creations, he (or more probably it will be she) is referred to "Plocacosmos; or, The Whole Art of Hairdressing," by James Stewart, 1782, wherein the mysteries of the art are set forth with great minuteness and elaboration, far too long to be explained here. The directions for the lady's "nightcap" may, however, be given:—

"All that is required at night is to take the cap or toke off, as any other ornament, and as you put them on, you can easily know how to take them off: with regard to the hair, nothing need be touched but the curls; you may take the pins out of them, and, with a little soft pomatum in your hands, stroke the hairs that may have started; do them with nice long rollers, wind them up to the roots, and turn the end of each roller firmly in to keep them tight, remembering at the same time the hair should never be combed at night, having always so bad an effect as to give a violent headache next day. After the curls are rolled up, touch them with your pomatumy hands, and stroke the hair behind; after that take a very large net fillet, which must be big enough to cover the head and hair, and put it on, and drawing the strings to a proper tightness behind, till it closes all round the face and neck like a purse, bring the strings round the front and back again to the neck, where they must be tied; this, with the finest lawn handkerchief, is night covering sufficient for the head."

"Heads" usually lasted a matter of three weeks, when—'twould be dangerous, madam, to delay longer the opening of your head. We get a glimpse of the possible state of a lady's head at the expiration of that time from the many recipes and advertisements for the destruction of insects in the magazines of the period, which reminds us of Julian, who likened his beard to a "forest grown populous with troublesome little animals."

> "Still to be neat, still to be drest,
> As you were going to a feast;
> Still to be powdered, still perfumed:
> Lady, it is to be presumed,
> Though art's hid causes are not found,

All is not sweet, all is not sound.
Give me a look, give me a face,
That makes simplicity a grace;
Robes loosely flowing, hair as free:
Such sweet neglect more taketh me,
Than all the adulteries of art;
They strike mine eyes, but not mine heart."

Ben Jonson, The Silent Woman.

The apeing by the tradespeople of the manners of the great is amusingly told in the *Lady's Magazine* for August, 1782, in the form of a letter to the editor, purporting to be from a respectable greengrocer, who signs himself "Artichoke Pulse." He says: "I wish to God you would write something smart against fashion. My family is almost ruined by the article of dress." It appeared that his son Tom had worked himself into a gentleman's family as footman, and from this circumstance his troubles began. "You can scarcely conceive, my dear Sir, what an alteration this acquaintance with the great family has made. Sally, my eldest daughter, talks of taste and the mode, aye faith, and the dresses too. I will give you a description of her going to see the new comedy of the 'East Indian' the other night, in company with her brothers and sisters, and a lord's footman, who presented them with orders for the two-shilling gallery.

LOUIS XVI., MARIE ANTOINETTE, AND THE DAUPHIN.

Engraved by Augustin de St. Aubin.

"Dick Dusty, the hairdresser's apprentice, who lives in a court near us, was sent for at two o'clock, and two pound of Sangwine's eightpenny-halfpenny powder being procured, with a proper quantity of grease, the operation of the head was begun among the cabbages, lettuces, turnips, carrots, peas, and beans that surrounded us. Dick, who was but a novice at his business, cut and slashed away until he had left just as much hair as he could conveniently dress, and then, having worked the grease and the flour into a kind of paste, he plaistered over the head, using his hand as a trowel, until it was fairly encrusted so as to hide the colour of the hair, or to deceive the eye into a belief that the head was a pudding bag turned inside out!

"As it was summer, my daughters chose to go without caps, and an artificial bouquet was stuck in the front of those puddings. The gowns were silk; but being purchased at a pawnbroker's they were not properly cut for the fashionable hoop. Hoops, however, were to be wore, and even my wife resolved for once, to figure away in one of those oval pieces of nonsense."

*　　　*　　　*　　　*　　　*

"Perhaps in nature, there was never such a figure! Only fashion to yourself a greengrocer's wife issuing from her cellar in Drury Lane, with a monstrous hoop, exposing a pair of legs, the ankles as thick as the calf, and the calf as thick as the modern waist; her hair bepuddened, her cheeks bedaubed with red, her neck of a crimson hue, her arms bursting through a pair of white gloves, the contrast between the two skins being almost the very opposite to each other; a thick-flowered silk exposing the whole front of a quilted petticoat that once was white, and then you have the appearance of my wife! Her daughters made as ridiculous a figure, and Will, I do assure you, was not the least remarkable in the group."

This sally, recounting the woes of the hapless "Artichoke," provoked an indignant reply from a champion of the women, which duly appeared in the next number: —

"I think it high time, then, for every female to exert the little knowledge she may be possessed of in the scribbling line, when the wits, under the characters of Green Grocers, dare to insult us, and speak of our hoops, and other parts of our dress, as freely as they exercise their authority over the ostlers at a country inn.

"The favour, dear Madam, we wish of you, is to remonstrate with these smart gentlemen, and, with us, tell them they are incapable of correcting the foibles in the ladies' dresses, till they have established a criterion for their own. Did they adopt no other fashions than useful and becoming ones, they might have some solid reasons for reprehending us; but how is this to be done? Can they point out of what use are the high-crowned hats, their shoes tied with strings, the number of buttons lately added to their coats: of what real service that ponderosity of their watches and canes? We will even attend to the Green Grocer, if he can defend them, and no longer despise the opinions of those scrutators of our dress; but till then we must insist that the hoop (the battery at which most of their present artillery is played off against), when of a moderate size, is an addition to the appearance of a fine woman; it is a finishing grace to their persons, and gives them that dignity of appearance that every woman in a genteel line of life has a right to assume."

Although Kings have often vainly endeavoured to impose their will upon the people in the matter of apparel it has often happened that monarchs have set the prevailing fashion of the period. This is especially noticeable in the Cavaliers of Charles I., numbers of whom adopted the short, pointed beard and moustachios and long hair of their master, in striking contrast to the close cropped and shaven round heads of the Cromwellians. It was so with the Bonapartists of the Third Empire, when the "imperial" became the vogue.

A REIGNING MONARCH.

At a still more recent period, the illustrious personage who is figured here, and who, be it known, appears here *strictly incognito* (we would fain escape the dire consequences of *lèse-majesté*), has imposed his imperious will, not only upon his own countrymen, but upon the world at large, in the matter of the turned up moustachio.

"When you come to be trimed, they will ask you whether you will be cut to looke terrible to your enimie, or amiable to your freend, grime and sterne in countenance, or pleasant and demure,—how their mowchatowes must be preserved and laid out, from one cheke to another, yea, almost from one eare to another, and turned up like two hornes towards the forehead" (Stubbes, "Anatomy of Abuses," 1583).

The angle at which it is pointed provides an index as to character, and of the degree of pugnacity of the wearer. At an angle of, say, 45 degrees forward we may expect to see its owner enter a crowded omnibus with the point of his umbrella held at the same angle, or as a soldier makes ready to present arms.

PHILIP IV. OF SPAIN.

In the dressing of the hair, as in costume generally, the lowest depth of the commonplace has been reached during the nineteenth century. It is, however, extremely dangerous to indulge in any kind of sweeping generalities with respect to our own epoch; we are either, from long habit and custom, prejudiced in favour of a particular *régime,* or we are afflicted with that contempt which is born of a too great familiarity. The chignon, in its many developments, is within the memory of most of us; the odious Piccadilly fringe still endures with those persons who are either slaves to habit or who find that the curling and frizzing of the hair of the forehead destroys its capacity for growth. Dundreary and mutton-chop whiskers are even now to be found in out-of-the-way country places. Goldsmith, in one of his delightful essays, tells a story of a traveller who, on his way to Italy, found himself in a country where the inhabitants had each a large excrescence depending from the chin—a deformity which, as it was endemic and the people little used to strangers, it had been the custom, time immemorial, to look upon as the greatest beauty. Ladies grew toasts from the size of their chins, and no men were beaux whose faces were not broadest at the bottom. It was Sunday; a country church was at hand, and our traveller was willing to perform the duties of the day. Upon his first appearance at the church door the eyes of all were fixed upon the stranger; but what was their amazement when they found that he actually wanted that emblem of beauty, a pursed chin! Stifled bursts of laughter, winks, and whispers circulated from visage to visage; the prismatic figure of the stranger's face was a fund of infinite gaiety. Our traveller could no longer patiently continue an object of deformity to point at. "Good folks," said he, "I perceive that I am a very ridiculous figure here, but I assure you I am reckoned no way deformed at home."

Lord Dundreary would have been impossible in any other epoch than the Victorian, although the Dundreary whisker is but a glorified development of earlier forms—

> "A marchaunt was ther with a forked berd,
> In motteleye high on horse he sat."

Canterbury Tales.

Dundreary, with his striped peg-tops, his eyeglass, and his drawl, exactly fitted his environment. His whiskers represent the very antithesis of the "Piccadilly fringe," also happily gone, or relegated to the coster fraternity, together with the bell-bottomed trouser with which it is in singular affinity.

The Piccadilly fringe was persistently condemned by artists, notably Mr. G. F. Watts, who pointed out that it obscured and destroyed the beautiful way in which the hair springs from the forehead. Mr. Watts, however, was not the first to warn the ladies against the sin of cropping short and pulling out the hair of the forehead. If there should, peradventure, be any fair readers who are enamoured of the beauties of either the Piccadilly or other fringe, or who should be smitten with the insane desire to pop, paint, or powder the face, let them listen to the sound advice and good counsel which the Knight of La Tour Landry gave to his daughters, and to the terrible "ensaumples" which he held up to them for their consideration and avoidance:

"Alas!" he exclaims, "whi take women non hede of the gret love that God hathe yeve hem to make hem after hys figure? and whi popithe they, and paintithe, and pluckithe her visage otherwise than God hath ordeined hem?" Why indeed! There was once a lady who died and suffered great tortures in hell, the devil holding her "bi the tresses of the here of her hede, like as a lyon holdithe his praie...." and the same "develle putte and thruste in her browes, temples, and forehede hote brenninge alles and nedeles"; and why was she subjected to all this torment? *Because she had "plucked her browes, front and forehed, to have awey the here, to make her selff the fayrer to the plesinge of the worlde."*

It is a very far cry from the good Knight of La Tour Landry to the wicked Mr. Punch of Fleet Street, who satirises the variations in the form of the short side whisker still beloved of butlers and ostlers, and which, in the early days of the Volunteer movement of the beginning of the sixties, became identified with particular regiments or companies:—

"Hairdresser: South Middlesex or Keveens, sir? (*Customer looks bewildered.*) Why, sir, many corpses, sir, 'as a rekignised style of 'air, sir, accordin' to the Reg— — (*Customer storms.*) Not a wolunteer, sir?—Jus' so, sir. Thought not, sir; leastways I was a-wonderin' to myself d'rectly I see you, what corpse you could a belonged to, sir."

X
BOOTS, SHOES, AND OTHER COVERINGS FOR THE FEET

'"Who is there in the house?' said Sam, in whose mind the inmates were always represented by that particular article of their costume which came under his immediate superintendence. 'There's a wooden leg in number six; there's a pair of Hessians in thirteen; there's two pair of halves in the commercial; there's these here painted tops in the snuggery inside the bar; and five more tops in the coffee-room.'

"'Nothing more?' said the little man.

"'Stop a bit,' replied Sam, suddenly recollecting himself. 'Yes; there's a pair of Wellingtons a good deal worn, and a pair o' lady's shoes in number five.'

"'What sort of shoes?' hastily inquired Wardle, who, together with Mr. Pickwick, had been lost in bewilderment at the singular catalogue of visitors.

"'Country make,' replied Sam.

"'Any maker's name?'

"'Brown.'

"'Where of?'

"'Muggleton.'

"'It is them!' exclaimed Wardle. 'By Heaven, we've found them.'"

Posthumous Papers of the Pickwick Club.

HEADING: SHOES (SEVENTEENTH AND EIGHTEENTH CENTURIES)

X

BOOTS, SHOES, AND OTHER COVERINGS FOR THE FEET

The good St. Crispin, of blessed memory, cobbling shoes for the poor by the light of his candle and filling up the interval with preaching, is a figure which all shoemakers regard with reverence. How did Crispin become the tutelary saint of shoemakers? Well, it was in this wise. Crispin, travelling with his brother Crispinian, in company with St. Denis, to Soissons in France to propagate the Christian faith, towards the close of the third century, in order that he might not be a burden to others for his maintenance, exercised at night the trade of shoemaker, preaching the Gospel by day. The shoes were sold at a low price to the poor, an angel (so the legend recounts) miraculously furnishing the leather. According to another version of the legend, the saint *stole* the leather, so as to enable him to benefit the poor. Crispin's efforts, like those of so many other benefactors of their kind, were poorly rewarded. He was ordered to be beheaded, and suffered martyrdom in 287 A.D., not, however, for his shoemaking, or for his thefts, but on account of his religious tenets. Some accounts state that he and his brother were flung into a cauldron of molten lead.

CLOG, OR PATTEN. FIFTEENTH CENTURY.

The brotherhood of the shoemakers has always included men of remarkable character and parts. Hans Sachs, born at Nuremburg in 1494, the most eminent German poet of his time; George Fox, first of Quakers, true follower of Crispin, dividing his time and energies between shoemaking and preaching; William Gifford, less remembered perhaps as a shoemaker than for his editorship of the famous *Quarterly*—these are a few only of the men "who have imparted a glory to the 'gentle craft,' as shoemaking has been called since the days of the illustrious Crispin," and invested it with distinction.[28]

The universal observance by Eastern nations of the custom of removing the shoes as a mark of reverence is in obedience to the command given to Moses from the burning bush at Horeb: "Put off thy shoes from off thy feet, for the place whereon thou standest is holy ground." The Western practice of uncovering the reverse end of the human anatomy presents a curious and somewhat startling contrast.

---

[28] Thomas Deloney's "booke called the Gentle Crafte, intreating of Showmakers," tells how Crispin and Crispianus, sons of King Logrid of Britain and of Queen Estreda, were sheltered at Faversham, Kent. Crispin wooed and married Princess Ursula, whose son was born in the shoemaker's house. Hence the saying, "A shoemaker's son is born a Prince." From their high lineage, shoemaking is named "The Gentle Craft."

> "I am of Crispin's trade, a brave Shooemaker,
> He loved a Princess dear, and ne'r forsak't her....
> This craft was never held in scorn, Sir Thomas Eyer did it adorn,
> A Shoemaker's son a Prince is born."

Roxburghe Ballads.

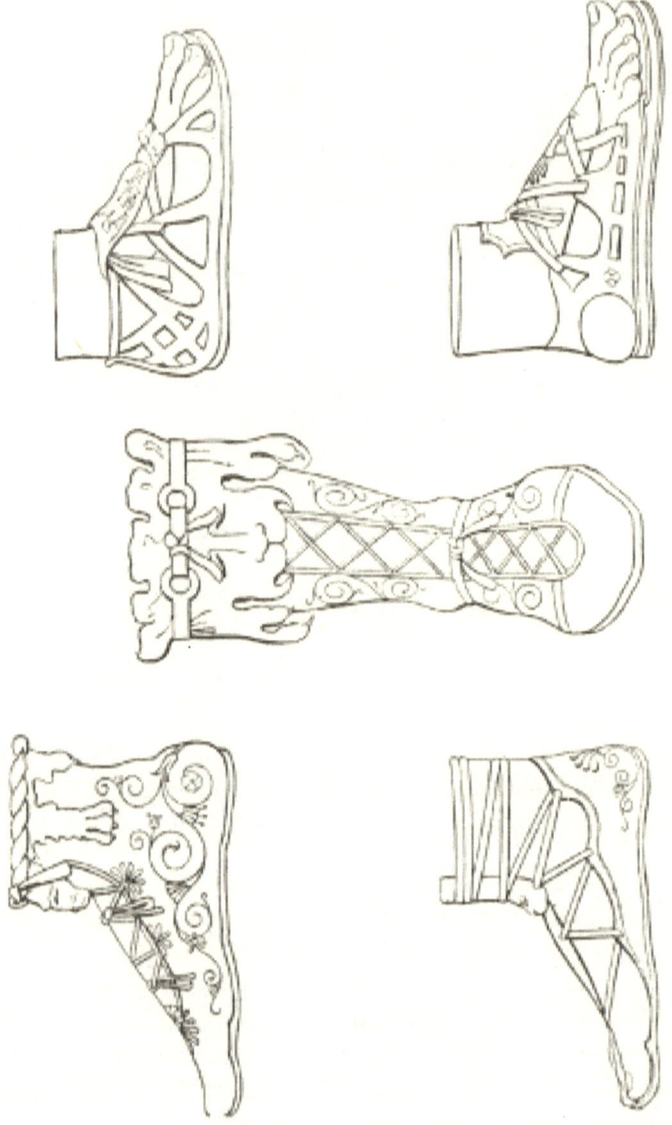

ROMAN SANDALS (HOPE'S "COSTUME OF THE ANCIENTS").

Hope's "Costume of the Ancients."

Footgear began as a protection to the *soles* of the feet, since it is the soles which necessarily demand some sort of protection until that time when the "rough places shall be made plain," although Nature provides her own protection to the soles of feet which are habitually bare, by thickening the skin. The skin of the habitually barefooted Irish lassie varies, we are told, from a quarter to half an inch in thickness, and even more.

The sandal, then, may be considered as the precursor of the shoe. Most of the early nations wore sandals. The Egyptians, however, were usually barefooted, with the exception of the priests, who wore shoes of *byblus*, and were not permitted to wear any other. The Greek sandal consisted of a strip of thick hide, tanned or untanned, for the sole, with a thinner piece, assuming some ornamental form, upon the instep, the whole connected or drawn together with straps drawn crosswise over the instep and round the ankle, or a cord or thong passing between the great toe and the first of the smaller toes.

Sandals were worn either with bare feet or with stockings or hose, in which case a division of the stocking would be necessary between the great and little toes. Some modern hygienic reformers have, indeed, recommended toed stockings for present use, *i.e.*, stockings provided with a separate receptacle for each toe, like the fingers of a glove, to be worn even with the modern shoe or boot, on the ground of healthiness, and this would seem to be reasonable, since the objectionable condition of the skin between the toes, which no amount of cleanliness and care can wholly avert, is due to the inability of the perspiration to escape when the surfaces are in contact. "The interposition in the five-toed socks of a layer of woollen or other material between each toe absorbs the perspiration and rapidly effects a remarkable change. The skin between the toes becomes dry and wholesome, and the squeezed, crippled appearance of the toes greatly alters for the better."[29]

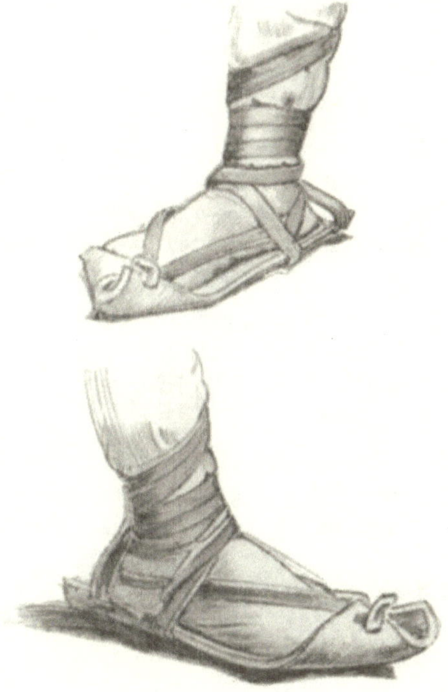

SANDALS OF THE ITALIAN PEASANTRY.

[29] "Health Culture," G. Jaeger, M.D.

Both the Greeks and Romans wore buskins, which reached to about the middle of the calf. These were variously ornamented and laced, and were usually lined with the skins of the smaller animals, the heads and claws being allowed to fall over the top by way of ornament. Buskins have, as a matter of fact, been worn at all periods; several examples are given, notably in the portraits by Vandyke, of Lords John and Bernard Stuart (p. 287).

The footgear of the Italian peasant of the present day may be considered as the most primitive form of sandal. It consists of a simple oblong piece of thick leather, perforated at the sides and ends to allow of straps being drawn through, crosswise over the instep and round the ankle, and half way up the leg, to the knee, either in circular bands or crosswise, the foot and leg being encased in a more or less loose stocking or hose, in many instances the whole of the leg being cross gartered.

The early Britons wore a shoe which was almost as simple in construction as the last mentioned. It consisted of a piece of raw cowhide, with a leather thong fastened at the heel, threaded along the upper edge, drawing the shoe like a purse over the foot. This form of shoe, however, was not confined to the early Britons, but was adopted by most primitive peoples at different periods; in fact, it is the first and readiest method of covering the feet which would occur to the primitive mind.

The Anglo-Saxon shoe was provided with long thongs of leather or other material attached to the shoe at the ankles and wound crosswise round the leg to the knee, or round the whole of the leg to the middle, always, however, with some form of hose. This fashion obtained, more or less, during the whole of the Anglo-Saxon period, and was common to most of the Northern nations.

During the reign of William the Conqueror, short boots reaching above the ankle, with a plain band round the tops, prevailed. Robert, Duke of Normandy, eldest son of the Conqueror, who died in 1134, was called "Curta Ocrea," or Short Boots, either from his setting the fashion or from retaining it when abandoned by the beaux of the day.

The usual footgear of the period, however, is the close shoe, made of cloth, velvet, leather, or other material, and terminating in a point. From this period for more than a century onward, shoes varied very little, except in the character of their ornamentation.

During the reigns of Henry II. and Richard I., a kind of loose top-boot appeared. These boots resembled loose socks or galoches, drawn over the hose, sometimes reaching as high as the knee, and occasionally to the middle of the thigh, but more often half way up the leg only. They were worn in various forms by all classes, and by the common people during a long period. They had no fastenings or lacings, but were allowed to fall at will, according to the stiffness or otherwise of the material of which they were made.

In the miniatures of the "Facta et Dicta Memorabilia" of Valerius Maximus, begun by Simon de Hesdin for Charles V. of France in 1375, and completed by Nicholas de Gonesse for Jean, Duc de Berry, in 1405, a number of figures have boots, made apparently of soft leather and coloured either red or white, reaching to the knee; in some instances the tops turned down, with long, pointed toes. This series of miniatures is extremely interesting as giving an insight into the domestic life of the fourteenth century, some of the interiors being especially so.

LORDS JOHN AND BERNARD STUART.

Engraved by James Macardell.

During the reign of the Plantagenets, footgear, like the rest of the costume of that period, was exceedingly sumptuous. The shoes were usually close-fitting, with pointed toes, and ornamented with the richest variety of patterning. The tops were of various materials, soft leather, silk, cloth, cloth-of-gold, &c. The soles were usually of thicker leather, but occasionally of wood, and even of cork. Upon the opening of the tomb of Henry VI. of Sicily, the dead monarch was discovered wearing shoes of which the uppers were of cloth-of-gold embroidered with pearls, and the soles of cork, covered with cloth-of-gold.

The reign of Richard II. was the period of abnormally long pointed toes, which occasionally reached the length of six inches and more, and assumed various shapes, the toes being stuffed with tow or other substance to keep them in shape.

This fashion of long pointed toes lasted during the three succeeding reigns. "Even boys wore doublets of silk, satin, and velvet; and almost all, especially in the Courts of Princes, had points at the toes of their shoes a quarter of an ell long and upwards, which they now called *poulaines*." Paradin describes the men as "wearing shoes with a point before, half a foot long: the richer and more eminent personages more than a foot, and Princes *two feet long*, which was the most ridiculous thing that ever was seen; and when men became tired of these pointed shoes, they adopted others in their stead denominated duck-bills, having a bill or beak before, of four or five fingers in length."

The sumptuary laws regulating these matters have been referred to in the introduction to this work. The Act of 3 Edward IV. restricted the length of toe to two inches.

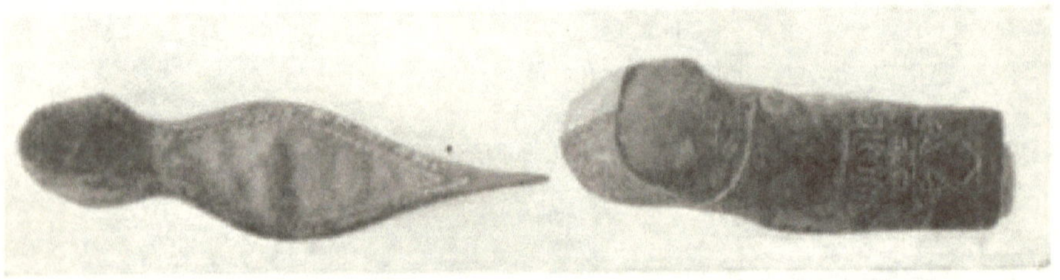

<table>
<tr><td>*French. Fifteenth Century.*</td><td>*French. Seventeenth Century.*</td></tr>
</table>

SHOES, FRENCH (FIFTEENTH AND SEVENTEENTH CENTURIES)

Clogs and pattens were worn from the time of Richard II. onwards as a protection to the soles of the shoes, and were variously shaped. Randal Holme calls *pattanes* "irons to be tied under the shoes to keep them out of the dirt." In an anonymous work called the "Eulogium," cited by Camden, it states: "Their shoes and pattens are snouted and piked, more than a finger long, crooking upwards, which they call *crackowes*, resembling devils' claws, and fastened to the knees with chains of gold and silver."

This fashion of appending chains to the peaks of the shoes lasted intermittently for a considerable time. In a work on "Ancient Costume," by Major Hamilton Smith, a portrait of James I. of Scotland is mentioned, in which the peaks of the monarch's shoes are fastened by chains of gold to his girdle.

There is a manuscript in the Royal collection in which the Duke of Gloucester, afterwards Richard III., is depicted as wearing a clog. This has been adopted by Abbey in his famous picture of "Gloucester and the Lady Anne."

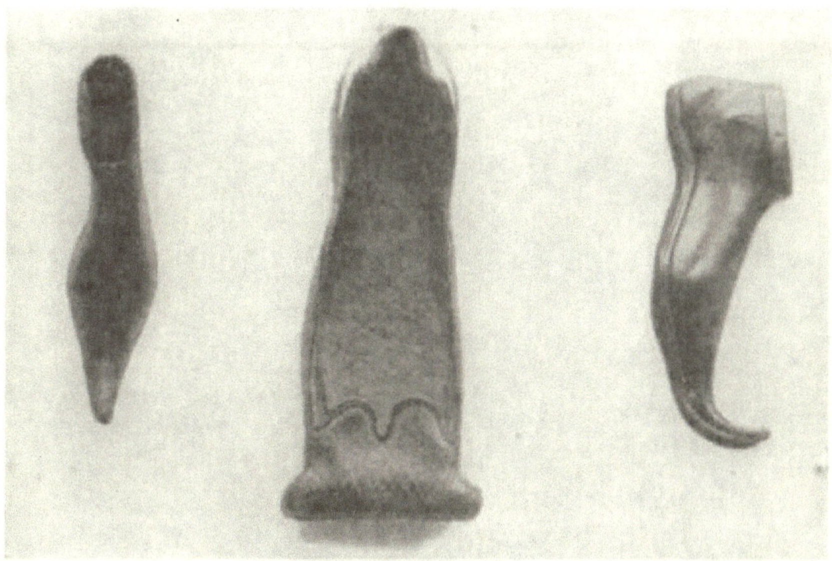

Child's Shoes, Front and Side View, German (Sixteenth Century).
Man's Shoe, German (Sixteenth Century).

SHOES, GERMAN (SIXTEENTH CENTURY)

Clogs were of wood, thickened at the heel and ball of the foot for the purpose of raising it from the ground. Afterwards it was further raised by means of two pieces set at right angles to the foot, on precisely the same principle as the Japanese shoes of to-day. An illustration is given from the Cluny Museum (p. 282).

Another means of raising the foot was the "chopine," which was a kind of stilt; it was, in fact, the sole, elongated to an extravagant degree. Hamlet thus addresses the lady players: "What! my young lady and mistress! By'r-lady, your ladyship is nearer heaven than when I saw you last, by the altitude of a chopine!"

Towards the close of the fifteenth century it became the fashion to bend the long toe over the shoe backwards. The two examples figured at the head of this chat are from the Cluny Museum, and are characteristic. Both have high heels, and resemble the shoes with which the Chinese ladies until quite recently tortured and mutilated their feet, for the purpose, it is said, of pleasing the distorted fancy of the men and to be qualified for marriage.[30]

---

[30] A movement, headed by the Empress, has been instituted recently for the abolition of the practice of mutilating the feet of Chinese women, which was universal throughout all classes of society. In the cities, ladies were carried through the streets pick-a-back, and moved about their houses on their knees. In the fields the women worked on their knees, being unable to stand.

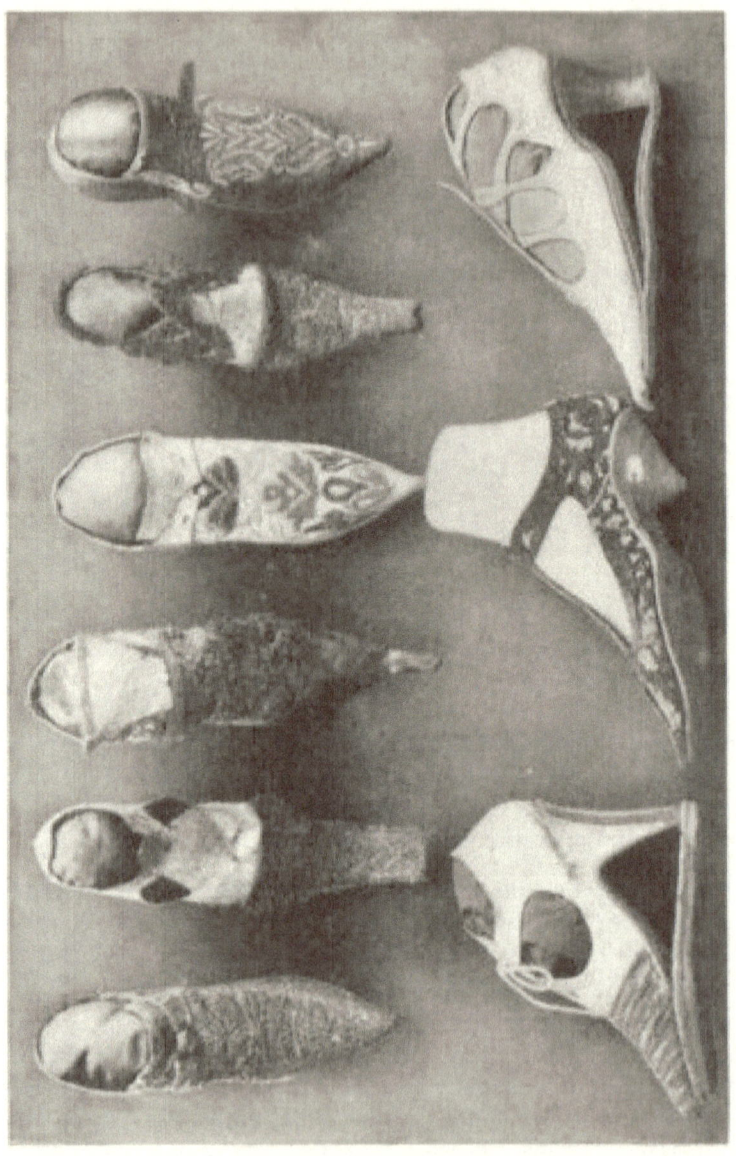

**SHOES OF THE SIXTEENTH AND SEVENTEENTH CENTURIES.
MUSÉE DE CLUNY.**

A number of examples of shoes of the fifteenth, sixteenth, and seventeenth centuries are given from the interesting collection in the Musée de Cluny, and will serve, far better than any written description, to give an idea of the character of the footgear of these periods. The two child's shoes given on p. 291 are of leather, and are typical of the shoe worn during the greater part of the fifteenth century. The side view shows the point turned upwards. The man's shoe is short-toed, richly worked in stamped leather. The ladies' shoes of the sixteenth and seventeenth centuries given on p. 293 are of various materials, and for the most part richly embroidered; two of the three lower ones show the clog of leather which was fixed from the heel to the toe, the centre one of the three having a sharp pointed heel and a rounded sole, surely a most uncomfortable thing to wear. Sir Thomas Parkins ("Treatise on Wrestling," 1714) says: "For shame, let us leave off aiming at the outdoing our Maker in our true symmetry and proportion; let us likewise, for our own ease, secure treading and upright walking, as He designed we should, and shorten our heels."

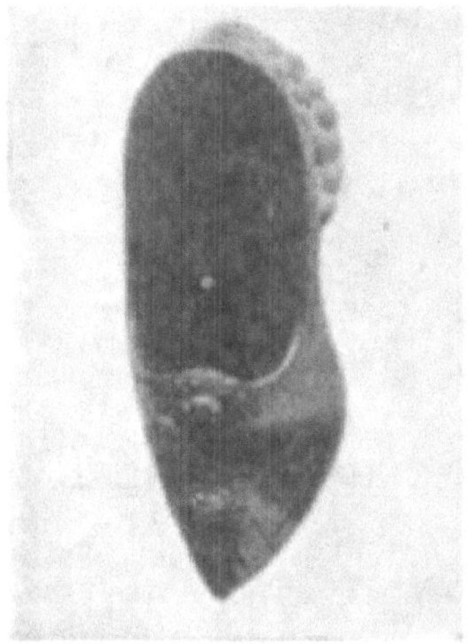

CARVED WOODEN SHOE, FRENCH (SEVENTEENTH CENTURY).

During the reign of the Tudors the character of the shoe suddenly changed from the long pointed toe to the broad-toed shoe, made either of various cloths, kid, or velvet, slashed and puffed with silk, an example of which will be seen in Holbein's picture of the "Two Ambassadors." The shoes of this period afford a minimum of protection to the feet, the whole of the instep being uncovered. It was again found necessary for legislation to step in—this time, however, to restrict their *breadth*, instead of the length of the toes, as heretofore.

Bulwer's "Pedigree of the English Gallant" says: "In the reign of Queen Mary, the people in general had laid aside the long points they formerly wore at the end of their shoes, and caused them to be made square at the toes, with so much addition to the breadth, that their feet exhibited a much more preposterous appearance than they had done in the former instance; therefore," says the author, "a proclamation was made, that no man should wear his shoes above six inches square at the toes." He then tells us that "picked shoes soon after came again in vogue, but they did not, I presume, continue any great time in use."

In the figure of the exquisite of 1670, after Mitelli (p. 129), the squareness of the toes is emphasised, the two corners even projecting from the flat edge. There are small bunches of ribbons at the toes, an abnormally large stiffened bow at the instep, and, by way of "piling Pelion upon Ossa," the bend of the stiffened bows is supplemented by smaller bows, representing the very acme of whimsical extravagance.

Usually these bows or ribbons were allowed to fall loose, in which case, however, they never reached such extravagant proportions as in the before-mentioned instance. A square-toed shoe of a Dutch officer of the Guards, 1662, is given, having a loose bow, also a shoe of a musketeer with a small buckle on the instep and a large tongue or flap in front.

SHOE, DUTCH OFFICER OF GUARDS, 1662.

Buckles have been worn from quite an early period, an example of a circular buckle occurring on a brass of 1376. They formed the usual fastening of the shoe during the Commonwealth, and were worn until the close of the eighteenth century, when they fell into disuse. The buckle-makers of 1800, alarmed at their declining trade, petitioned the Prince of Wales to discard his new strings and adopt the buckle, but, although the Prince complied with the wishes of the petition, it was of no avail.

Buckles were often richly jewelled, and consequently very costly. Those worn by the Hon. John Spencer on the occasion of his marriage were said to be worth £30,000.

SHOE OF A MUSKETEER, MOUSQUETAIRE, 1697.

In the anonymous portrait of Prince Henry, eldest son of James I. (p. 103), the shoes are of leather, slashed, showing the coloured stocking underneath, and otherwise ornamented, with the strap drawn over the instep, covered by a jewelled rosette, or "shoe-rose." These shoe-roses had a great vogue during the time of Elizabeth; they were usually of bunches of ribbons made to form a rose, and were occasionally ornamented with costly jewels.

"With two Provencal roses on my razed shoes."

Hamlet, Act III, sc. 2.

In "Hæc-Vir, or the Womanish Man," 1621, is described a fashionable man, who "takes a full survey of himself, from the highest sprig in his feather to the lowest spangle that shines in his shoe-string."

We now come to the period of high-topped boots, which continued with variations to the time of George II. In the portrait of Charles I. by Daniel Mytens in the National Portrait Gallery will be seen an example of the earlier form of top-boot. The tops fit close, and are turned down at the knee, and the edges again turned up half-way down the calf of the leg. A large flap with double edges protects the instep.

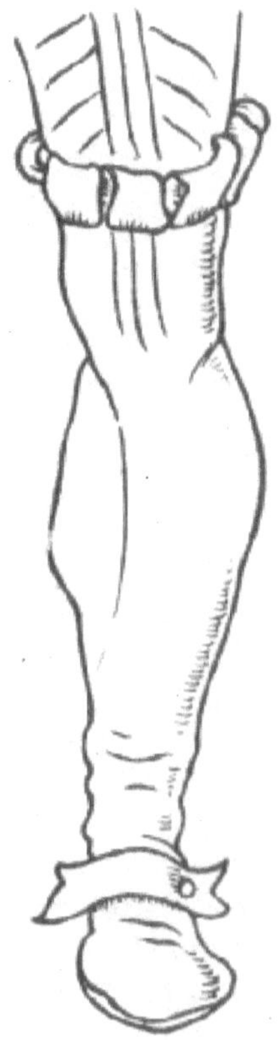

TOP BOOT, LOUIS XIII., 1611.

The form of top-boots was developed in various ways, until it reached an extravagant pitch in France in the reign of Louis XIV. The variations were mainly in the shape or adjustment of the tops, rather than in that portion of the boot which covered the foot. They were worn by the dandies with a profusion of costly lace. Several examples are given.

This was the period of the highest, or rather widest, development of the tops of the boots; so wide, indeed, did they become, that the gait of a man might be described as straddling rather than walking.

An example is given of a boot worn by the Comte de Soissons, 1628, which has a stiff rounded top like a basin, with a short hose worn over the hose proper, turned down below the knee and edged with rich lace.

A variation of the top-boot worn from the time of Elizabeth onwards is a kind of soft leather hose or buskin drawn up to the middle of the thigh, the edge folded over and slashed; these were worn during the slashed period, when everything was slashed—hat, sleeves, doublet, and tunic (p. 297).

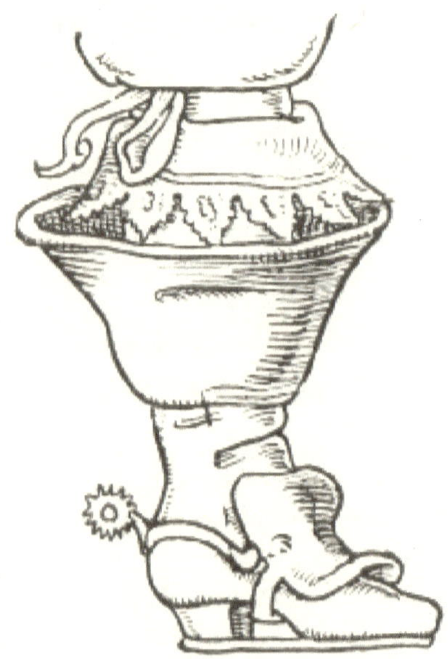

TOP BOOT, COMTE DE SOISSONS, 1628.

The "Wellington" boot of the present day is practically identical with that worn by the illustrious soldier from whom it takes its name, and is a very slight variation of the form of riding boot which was in use at the beginning of the eighteenth century, except that it is of softer leather, allowing the boot to fall into folds at the ankle. The boot in the portrait of Napoleon by Isabey, in the Musée de Versailles, may be described as a sort of half Wellington, but the top-boot which is usually associated with Napoleon is cut away at its upper edge at the back, the front forming a kind of mask to the knee, a form of boot which, in fact, had been worn from the time of William III.

BRAVOES (MARTIN SCHONGAUER).

Martin Schongauer.

Cloth and woollen boots and shoes, as were worn in the Middle Ages, have been recommended for *modern* wear as being more healthy, and as allowing the natural perspiration of the foot to exhale, their sponsors affirming that "cloth and wool are perfectly suitable and safe for wet weather, as the wetting of the wool does not chill the feet, the heat of which promptly evaporates the moisture from the covering, which soon dries." It must, however, be admitted that with a cloth covering, the dirt and mud of a London winter would be a trial, and here, doubtless, we have a reason for the cobblestones of mediæval towns. Cobble-stones are clean, but must at once be ruled out of the question for London. Cobble-stones would indeed add a fresh horror to London life. But is it too much to expect the richest city in the world, with its thousands of unemployed, to keep its streets clean? Is there any reason why large cities should not be kept clean as well as small cities?

"Boots and shoes should be roomy, to prevent the toes from being squeezed together, and should be so made that the great toe is not pressed against its neighbours, but is encouraged to lie in a straight line drawn from the heel to the root of the great toe. The heel of the boot should be low and broad."[31]

The Greek ideal of the foot is the true one. The Greeks rightly regarded the foot as an undeveloped hand, and they endeavoured in their sculpture to impart that hand-like character to their feet. One has only to notice the flexible toes of new-born and young babies, in order to perceive the reasonableness of this position. The Greeks in their sculpture made a distinct division between the great toe and the rest of the toes, as between the thumb and the fingers of the hand—the three toes well forward in a bunch; the first the longest, the next a little shorter, and the third shorter still; the little toe by itself, raised up. Now compare with this any natural foot habituated to shoes or boots. The bunch of three toes is pressed back, and also sideways against the great toe, thus losing the division between them and the great toe, and destroying the true contour of the foot. The pads of all the toes are pressed sideways instead of being immediately under the nails, and the foot has entirely lost its original character, and has become grotesquely malformed by corns, bunions, and similar growths. The most beautiful natural foot, the *only* beautiful foot which we ever remember having seen, was a cast in Sir Edgar Boehm's studio of the foot of a black woman who had never worn shoes.

Of late there has been a disposition to return to the sandal as a covering or rather protection for children's feet (one fears that it will be long before grown-ups adopt the sandal, except perhaps at the seaside or in the country). The change is a healthy one from every point of view. Upon æsthetic grounds it is especially welcome. One walks along the street during the summer months, the mind perhaps preoccupied, and the eye suddenly lights upon the rosy feet of one of these little ones as they trip along the street. One involuntarily exclaims, "What a charming design! What a beautiful piece of ornament!" Of a truth, in place of the uninteresting product of the shoemaker, which we had become so inured and accustomed to, one is suddenly introduced to that masterpiece of the Great Designer, the human foot, and the foot, too, in its natural state, before it has become crippled and distorted by long confinement in a leather prison.

---

[31] "Health Culture," G. Jaeger, M.D.

Lector House believes that a society develops through a two-fold approach of continuous learning and adaptation, which is derived from the study of classic literary works spread across the historic timeline of literature records. Therefore, we aim at reviving, repairing and redeveloping all those inaccessible or damaged but historically as well as culturally important literature across subjects so that the future generations may have an opportunity to study and learn from past works to embark upon a journey of creating a better future.

This book is a result of an effort made by Lector House towards making a contribution to the preservation and repair of original ancient works which might hold historical significance to the approach of continuous learning across subjects.

HAPPY READING & LEARNING!

LECTOR HOUSE LLP
E-MAIL: lectorpublishing@gmail.com